COMPLETE GUIDE TO
Embroidery
Stitches

COMPLETE GUIDE TO
Embroidery
Stitches

Photographs, Diagrams, and
Instructions for Over 260 Stitches

Embroidery by Jennifer Campbell
and Ann-Marie Bakewell

R eader's
Digest

The Reader's Digest Association, Inc.
Pleasantville, New York/Montreal/Sydney/Hong Kong

CONTENTS

HOW TO USE THIS BOOK

Stitching is one of the oldest crafts—needles were in everyday use in Europe before 20,000 BC—and has long been used for decorative as well as practical purposes. Over the years, a large number of stitches have been created, some with very specific uses and others that have much wider application. The 263 stitches in this book include all the basic stitches as well as those commonly used today.

Each stitch is presented in a close-up photograph so that you know exactly what the stitch looks like, along with a description of its main uses and easy-to-follow instructions for stitching it, including clear diagrams. Explanations and tips to help you achieve the best results complete each entry.

One problem with stitches is their names. There is no standardization, and any stitch may be known by a number of names. As many alternatives as possible are given and included in the index.

This book is divided into five main chapters. "Starting to embroider" deals with the basics to get you started: the fabrics, threads, and needles to use for each type of stitching, as well as an explanation of how to follow a pattern and basic embroidery stitching techniques, such as beginning and ending your threads. If you are just learning to embroider, you will find this chapter invaluable.

The next three chapters deal with the three main types of embroidery and the stitches that are used for each. "Embroidery on fabric" covers all surface, or freestyle, embroidery, including counted-thread work and beadwork. The main types of surface embroidery are explained, and then the stitches are presented in thirteen groups to help you find your way through them. "Smocking" covers the basics of smocking and the most commonly used smocking stitches. "Embroidery on canvas" explains how to work on canvas and then presents eight groups of canvas stitches.

Finally, there is a chapter on what to do once you have finished your embroidery. It includes suggestions for how to best display your work and information on how to care for it so that it will last for many years.

You can use this book in a number of ways, depending on your level of expertise:

● To look up a particular stitch, go to the index, which will refer you directly to the relevant page.

● To select a stitch for a particular project, go to the relevant chapter ("Embroidery on fabric," "Smocking," or "Embroidery on canvas"), and then to the section containing suitable stitches. Flick through, studying the photographs until you find a stitch you like.

● If you are just beginning to stitch, begin with the basics in "Starting to embroider." Decide on the type of embroidery you want to do (fabric, smocking, or canvas) and read the general instructions at the beginning of the appropriate chapter. Read the introduction to the group of stitches and then follow the instructions for the particular stitch you want to use.

● You can also simply browse through the stitches for pleasure and inspiration.

Left-handed embroiderers

Left-handed embroiderers should work in the opposite direction to the instructions given in the book: left to right where it says right to left, and vice versa, and wrap or loop the thread in the opposite direction to the one specified. Stitches worked from top to bottom, however, should still be worked from top to bottom.

STARTING TO
embroider

Although the following stitches are the basis of
all embroidery, the finished items depend on a
combination of stitches, fabrics, threads,
design, and skillful execution.

FABRICS

Embroidery can be worked on most fabrics, although some types of embroidery require specific types. Traditionally, linen was the choice of most embroiderers, as it is strong and retains its shape well. Choose a fabric that complements the embroidery, particularly for surface embroidery where the fabric is part of the final effect.

Fabric shrinkage can ruin embroidery, so wash the fabric before you begin stitching.

Plainweave fabrics

Plainweave fabrics are tightly woven, so the weave is not particularly obvious. They are used for surface, or freestyle, embroidery, where the stitches are worked without regard to the threads of the fabric. Some commonly used fabrics for embroidery are fine cottons (such as batiste, voile, and muslin/cheesecloth), damask, linens, silks, organza, and satin.

Although most embroidery is stitched on plain fabrics, patterned ones can also be used to good effect if the pattern suits the embroidery. Those with regular stripes, checks, or dots can also be used for stitches normally worked by counting threads.

Loosely woven, stretch, and synthetic fabrics may have to be stabilized before they are used for embroidery: a stabilizer such as dressmaker's interlining or water-soluble paper is applied to the back of the fabric, the design is stitched through both layers, and then the stabilizer is removed.

Evenweave fabrics

Evenweave fabrics are those in which the weave is regular—they have an equal number of warp and weft threads—and are used when stitches are worked by counting threads. The number of threads per 1 in. (2.5 cm) is known as the "count": 8 count means eight threads to 1 in. (2.5 cm) and so is a fairly coarse fabric. Evenweave fabrics include:

evenweave linen or cotton
comes in 18 to 36 count;
Aida cloth
has threads that form "squares" and comes in various sizes (from 8 to 18 count);
Hardanger cloth
has pairs of threads and comes in two sizes (22 and 24 count);
single-weave linen
is a single weave and comes in 10 count.

Canvas

Canvas is a strong fabric used for canvas work (see p. 172). Waste canvas, which is water-soluble and can be removed later, is used when working counted-thread stitches on plainweave fabrics.

voile

Hardanger

evenweave linen

plainweave linen

14-count Aida

canvas

silk   rayon   Danish flower thread   metallic thread   pearl cotton   broder cotton

THREADS

There are a number of different embroidery threads, and each has specific characteristics. The threads for a particular piece are selected depending on the fabric, the type of embroidery, and the stitches being used.

Cotton threads

Cotton threads are a very popular choice for embroidery.

Stranded embroidery cotton

or floss, is the thread most commonly used for embroidery. It can be used for surface embroidery, smocking, or finer forms of canvas work. It comes in a skein of six strands, and different types of embroidery may require one or more strands to be used. Work in lengths of no more than 16 inches

(40 cm) or the thread will lose its sheen.

Pearl cotton

or coton perlé, is a shiny 2-ply thread that is twisted so that it does not separate as you work. It is used for many different types of embroidery, including cross-stitch, smocking, and canvas work, and comes in a variety of thicknesses (3, 5, 8, and 12, with 3 being the thickest).

Broder cotton

or broderie cotton, is a soft, twisted (nondivisible) cotton suitable for all types of embroidery. Sizes 16 and 20 come in a range of colors; size 25 (the finest) comes only in white or ecru.

Flower thread

is a nondivisible cotton thread that has a very

Persian wool

Medici wool

crewel wool

tranded cotton

tapestry wool

low sheen and is often used for embroidery on linen. One strand equals two strands of stranded cotton.

Silk threads

Silk threads are very strong and do not break easily. They come in a wide range of types.
Stranded silk
is used in the same way as stranded cotton, but it has a greater sheen. It comes in a skein of four or six strands.
Flat, untwisted filaments of silk
are used for fine embroidery.
Heavy, nondivisible twisted silks
are also available.

Silk threads do not always hold color well and are not colorfast. They are not washable and fade quickly in direct sunlight, so store threads and embroideries in a dark place. Color may vary from one dye lot to another, so buy enough thread for an entire project in the same dye lot.

Rayon threads

Rayon (artificial silk) threads give the same shiny effect as silk threads. They are cheaper to buy but can be difficult to use. Dampening the thread by moistening your fingers and running them down the thread will help, and placing the threads in the freezer for a few hours will reduce static electricity.

Always strip the threads and use short lengths (see Helpful hint on p. 23).

Metallic threads

Metallic threads come in gold, silver, copper, and multicolors, in a variety of weights and textures. They are expensive and were traditionally used only for details, but cheaper synthetic ones are now widely available. Use only short lengths of these threads, as they wear easily and can be difficult to work with.

Wool threads

Wool threads are hard-wearing and are often used for embroidered upholstery, wall hangings, and pillows.

Crewel wool
or French wool, is a fine 2-ply wool used for crewel embroidery and canvas work, where strands may be combined for better coverage.

Tapestry wool
is a twisted, nondivisible 4-ply yarn used for embroidery and canvas work.

Persian wool
comes in three 2-ply strands that can be separated as required. It is thicker than crewel wool but finer than tapestry wool.

Medici wool
is a very thin embroidery wool, finer than crewel wool.

Rug wool
is a heavy, hard-wearing yarn used when making canvas-work rugs.

Some knitting yarns
may also be used for coarser work.

Blocking

The embroidery fabric or canvas may become distorted while you are stitching, especially if you are using a lot of diagonal stitches. To restore it to its original shape, it has to be blocked, which involves stretching it back to its original shape.

You will need a board large enough for the entire piece. Staple clean muslin (cheesecloth) or other fine cotton cloth over the board and mark a grid 1 inch or 1 ½ in. (2 or 3 cm) square on the cloth. Use a permanent marking pen and check that the ink will not run when damp. Alternatively, you can use a checked fabric such as gingham.

The blocking will be easier if it can be done while the fabric or canvas is damp. Check that it is shrink-proof and that the thread dyes are colorfast. If so, soak the piece in cold water, place facedown on the board (faceup for raised embroidery so the stitches are not crushed), and gently stretch it to shape over the grid. Use rust-proof push pins, straight pins, or tacks to hold it in shape, starting at the center lines and working out to the corners.

Allow the piece to dry and then remove it from the board. If necessary, repeat the process.

NEEDLES

Different types of embroidery require different types of needles. Those used most often are the following.

Crewel needles
are medium-length needles with a sharp point and a fairly large, long eye. They are used for most embroidery on plainweave fabrics. Sizes range from 1 to 10, with 1 being the largest.

Chenille needles
are sharp-pointed needles, larger and thicker than crewel needles and with a larger eye. They are used with heavier fabrics and thicker threads, such as crewel wool and six strands of cotton floss. Sizes range from 14 to 26, with 14 being the largest.

Tapestry needles
are medium-length needles with a blunt end and a long eye. They are used on evenweave fabrics and for canvas work to avoid splitting the fabric or canvas threads. They come in a range of sizes from 14 to 26, with 14 being the largest.

Straw, or milliner's, needles
have a straight shank that does not taper as most needles do and an eye that is no wider than the shank. They are useful for making bullion and knot stitches and can be used for beading. They come in a range from 1 to 11, with 1 being the largest.

Beading needles
are very long and fine, with a small eye. They

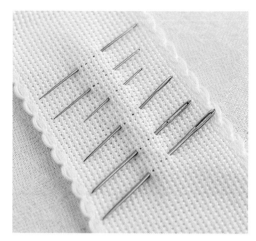

Crewel (three top) and tapestry (three bottom) needles.

are used when threading beads but bend easily and should be used carefully.

The size of the needle you use is important. The eye should be large enough to contain the thread, so that it is not damaged when the needle is pushed through the fabric, but not too large or the thread will not fill the hole made by it.

HELPFUL HINT
The eye of a needle is created by punching it out of the metal, so one side is larger than the other. If you are having trouble threading a needle, turn it around and try the other side! It also helps to moisten the end of the thread and press it flat between your fingers.

HOOPS AND FRAMES

Embroidery hoops and frames are used to hold the fabric taut so that it is not distorted as you work on it. Stitching may be slower, however, as you need to use the "stab" method of stitching (see p. 22).

Hoops consist of two rings: The fabric is placed over the smaller inner ring, and the larger outer ring is then placed on top. The larger ring has an adjustable screw that is gradually loosened until it fits neatly over the fabric. Don't tighten the screw over the fabric or the fabric will be distorted.

Winding cotton cloth around the hoops before you start will prevent them from marking the fabric. Remove the hoop each time you finish stitching so that it does not distort the fabric. When using a hoop, do not touch the fabric in the hoop; hold the hoop itself.

Frames are used less often but are useful for larger pieces. The fabric is stretched over the frame and held in place by lacing or with rustproof thumbtacks or staples.

HELPFUL HINT

A thimble can be used to protect your finger when you are stitching. Use it on the middle finger of your left hand (or your right hand if you are left-handed).

USING DESIGNS AND CHARTS

Embroidery designs can be transferred to fabric or canvas in many ways, depending on the fabric and embroidery technique being used. Some of the more popular methods are described on the following pages.

Iron-on transfers

Iron-on transfers are an easy way to transfer a design to fabric but they leave permanent marks and must be completely covered by embroidery. They work best on fabrics with a smooth surface, such as fine cottons. Follow the manufacturer's instructions on the packaging.

If you prefer to make your own transfer, trace the design onto heavy tracing paper using an ordinary pen or pencil.

1. Turn the tracing over and retrace the design using a special heat-transfer pen or pencil.

2. Pin the fabric, right side up, over a padded board such as an ironing board. Position the transfer on it, heat-transfer side down, and press firmly over each part of the design with a hot iron, as shown at right. (Don't slide the iron over the design.)

3. Carefully lift one corner of the paper to check that the design has been transferred. If not, continue pressing with the iron but don't scorch the fabric!

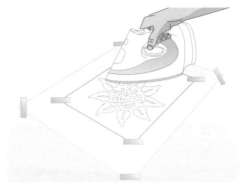

Press the iron firmly over the transfer.

The finished transfer.

Direct tracing

A design can be directly traced onto a light-colored, relatively sheer fabric or canvas. Tape the design to a flat surface and place the fabric or canvas over it. Again use tape to hold it in place and then trace over the design with a pencil.

The design and fabric can also be taped to a window to make it easier to see the lines.

Tracing will be easier if design and fabric are taped to a window.

Waterproof fabric-marking pens can be used, but these lines must be entirely covered by the embroidery.

Water-erasable pens are useful for washable fabrics, since any traces can be removed when the embroidery is finished.

Chalk-based fabric pencils brush or wash off easily and can be used on washable fabrics. As the chalk may brush off quickly, it can be useful to baste with thread over the lines to preserve the design.

Dressmaker's carbon paper

Using dressmaker's carbon paper is another option for tracing. It is suitable for smooth fabrics. The lines may be permanent, so the color selected should blend with the embroidery or be covered by it.

Place the carbon paper over the fabric and then position the design on top. Tape all three layers in place and draw over the design with a sharp lead pencil.

Water-soluble paper or film

Water-soluble paper or film can also be used to transfer a design. Print or trace the required design onto the water-soluble material and then baste it to the fabric, as shown below. Stitch the embroidery through the paper. Then follow the manufacturer's instructions to remove the paper and take out the tacking stitches.

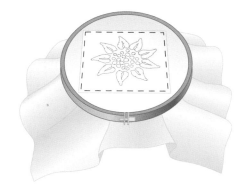

Stitch the embroidery through water-soluble paper.

Adjusting the size

If your chosen design is not the correct size, you can enlarge or reduce it on a photocopier or scan it into a computer and adjust the size. You can then transfer it to the fabric by one of the methods above.

Remember, though, if you are enlarging or reducing by a considerable amount, you may need to adjust the amount of detail in the design to get the result you want.

Charts

Designs for evenweave fabric and canvas are usually shown by means of a chart with a regular grid. Different threads and/or stitches are shown by different colors or symbols, and a key is provided to explain what each color or symbol means (see chart on p. 42).

Center lines are usually shown on the chart. They are used to center the design on the fabric. To find the center of the piece of embroidery fabric, fold it in half both ways and baste along the fold lines. Where they cross is the center of the fabric. These basting lines also correspond to the center lines on the chart and will provide a guide when you are counting stitches. If the design is not to be centered on the fabric, baste the lines wherever they will be appropriate so that you have the same guidelines to follow.

There are two types of charts: box charts and line charts:

In a box chart

each square of the grid represents one stitch. Thus it corresponds to one Aida cloth square, one canvas thread or one or two linen threads. If a stitch is to cover more than one square/thread, the grid squares are surrounded by a heavy line.

The two charts below show the same motif represented by colors or symbols.

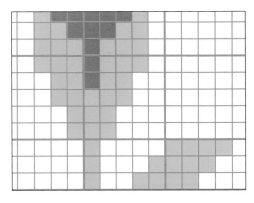

The design may be indicated by colored squares.

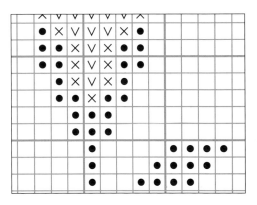

Symbols can be used to indicate each colored thread.

In a line chart

the lines of the grid correspond to the threads of the fabric or canvas and the stitches are shown by thick lines. This method gives the precise position of each stitch and is useful for more elaborate designs.

If a design is symmetrical or repeated, a

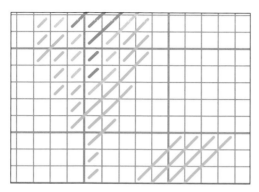

Colored lines show the position of each stitch.

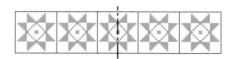

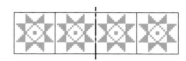

Position motifs according to the center line of the border.

chart may be given for only part of the design. If it is repeated, for example along a border, working from the chart will not be a problem, although you will need to be careful to space the designs consistently. Count the number of threads available and find the center line of the border. Work out how the motif will fit neatly, adjusting the number of background threads if necessary. Start work at the center: If there will be an odd number of motifs, center one on the center line; if there will be an even number of motifs, place one either side of the center line (see the diagrams above right).

If only part of a symmetrical design has been given, work the charted part first. You may then be able to turn the chart around to work the rest of the design. If the uncharted part is a mirror-image of the part given, you should work it in reverse.

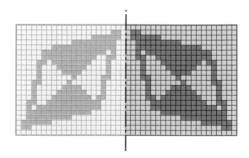

Symmetrical designs may include a mirror image.

BASIC STITCHING TECHNIQUES

Preparing the fabric

Before you start stitching, prepare your fabric:
- Check that it is shrinkproof and colorfast.
- Ensure you have a large enough piece to contain the whole design and leave a comfortable margin for a border around all sides.
- Allow for any extra fabric that will be needed when finishing the item. If a piece is to be framed or mounted, leave at least 2 in. (5 cm) all around.
- Prevent the edges from fraying by hemming around the piece. Don't use tape to bind the edges, as the adhesive may discolor the fabric and attract dirt.

Threading a needle

1. Cut the end of the thread cleanly at an angle.
2. Moisten the cut end, ensuring that it is the top end with the grain running down the thread. (If you try to push the thread through the eye against the grain, it will frizz up.) To find the grain, run the thread between your fingers. It will be much smoother with the grain.
3. Choose a needle with an eye that is large enough for the thread so that the thread does not get worn as it is pulled through the holes in the fabric.
4. Push the thread through the eye. If you are having trouble, reverse the eye, as one side is larger than the other. A needle threader can be used if desired.

Stitch methods

There are two methods of stitching, the sewing method and the stab method.

The sewing method is the faster, although it can be less accurate. It is the method used for the fabric and smocking-stitch diagrams in this book. Insert the needle and bring it out in one movement.

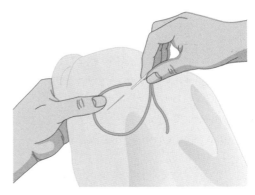

The sewing method requires no hoop.

HELPFUL HINT

You may find it easier to thread wools and thicker threads by the loop method. Fold the end of the wool around the eye of the needle and press it firmly. Slide the loop off the needle and then push the loop through the eye.

The stab method
allows the needle to be placed precisely. It is the method used with a hoop or frame and for canvas work. Insert the needle at a right angle to the fabric and push it through. Then insert it from the back and again push it through to the top.

The stab method allows more precise stitching.

Beginning and ending a thread

The embroidery thread must be held securely in the work so that your stitches do not come undone, but you do not want untidy knots and threads on the back of your work. There are several methods of beginning and ending a thread, depending on the type of embroidery you are stitching.

Back stitches
provide a secure beginning and ending and are useful for embroidery on clothes or linen that will be washed. To begin, work two tiny back stitches where they will be covered by the

embroidery, splitting the first stitch with the second to make them very secure. To end, work two tiny back stitches on the wrong side of the fabric. Cut off any tails of thread.

Waste knots
can also be used to begin most embroidery, especially where the starting point will not be concealed, as for canvas work or shadow work. Knot the end of the thread and take the needle through to the back of the fabric about 1 ¼ in. (3 cm) back from the starting point of the stitching. Bring the needle through to the front at the starting point of the stitching and work several stitches, working over the thread at the back of the fabric. Then cut off the knot and keep working. Use the weaving method to end.

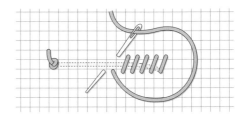

A waste knot can be used to begin most threads.

Waste back stitches
can be used when the embroidery will not cover a thread, for example with curving line stitches. Begin about 1 ¼ in. (3 cm) beyond the start of the embroidery and make several

small back stitches, leaving a tail of thread at least 2 in. (5 cm) long. Complete the stitches and use the weaving method (see below) to end. Then unpick the back stitches and use the weaving method to secure the thread on the back side.

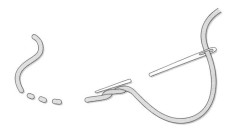

Waste back stitches hold the thread and are later unpicked.

Weaving

is the simplest method of ending the thread. After completing the stitching, take the needle and thread through the back of the stitches and run it through several stitches before clipping the thread close to the fabric.

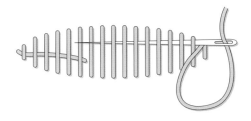

Weaving is a useful way to end a thread.

HELPFUL HINT

To separate stranded cottons, silks, or wools, first cut a length approximately 18 in. (46 cm) long from the skein. Take one strand and pull it from the group; then pull a second strand out and so on.

If you are using two or more strands, separate all of the six strands and then combine the required number again. They will lie more neatly once they are untwisted.

Working comfortably

You will gain greater enjoyment from working your embroidery if you are comfortable while working on it. Sit in a chair that has good support for your back and is the right height, so your feet are flat on the floor. Have all your materials within easy reach on a nearby table.

Keep all your tools and materials in a sewing box or bag and arrange your threads neatly by color in small containers.

Work in a well-lit area where you can see the threads clearly. Daylight is ideal, but avoid bright sunlight, glare may reflect from light-colored fabric. At night or on dull days, use a bright light, positioned so that your stitching hand does not produce a shadow over your work.

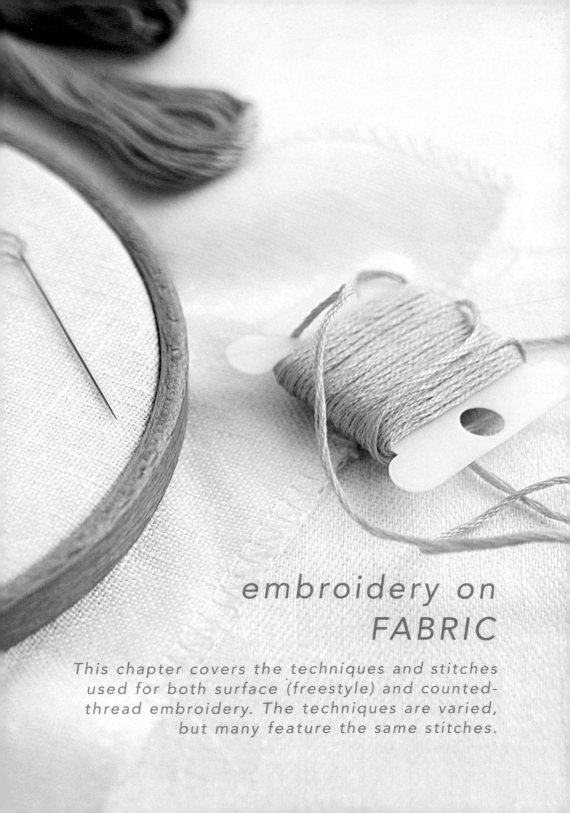

embroidery on FABRIC

This chapter covers the techniques and stitches used for both surface (freestyle) and counted-thread embroidery. The techniques are varied, but many feature the same stitches.

SURFACE EMBROIDERY

Surface embroidery, also known as freestyle embroidery, can be worked on any fabric, plainweave or evenweave, as it is worked without regard to the fabric threads. The design is usually applied directly to the fabric or worked by eye (see pp. 17–18).

Before you begin the embroidery, prepare your fabric and select threads. Work a small sample piece to check that they will produce the result you want in terms of both coverage and color (see pp. 12–14).

Surface embroidery is normally worked with a crewel needle, although tapestry needles are sometimes preferable, especially for stitches worked without piercing the fabric. Straw needles are useful for bullion stitches with a lot of wraps.

Using an embroidery hoop or frame to hold the fabric firmly while you are stitching will ensure that the design is not distorted.

Some of the main techniques are described in the following pages. They include crewel work, cutwork, drawn-thread work, and shadow work.

Crewel work

Crewel work, also known as Jacobean embroidery, developed in Europe in the seventeenth century and was used to decorate the wall hangings and upholstery fabrics that were increasing in popularity

Foliage and other curving shapes are characteristic of crewel embroidery.

at the time. It was worked using fine wool thread on hard-wearing wool, cotton, or linen fabrics, and the colorful designs were often elaborate, usually consisting of flowers, fruits, animals, and other graceful, curving shapes. The designs have a worked outline and separate filling, and the background is left unstitched. Crewel work enjoyed renewed popularity in the later nineteenth century as part of the art needlework movement.

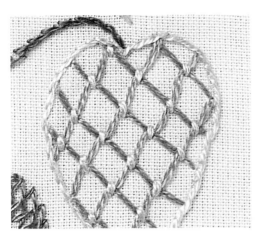

Trellis stitch is often used as a filling stitch in crewel work.

Modern embroiderers have adapted the technique and now apply the characteristic designs to any plainweave fabric, using cotton or silk threads as well as the traditional crewel wool.

Crewel needles, as the name implies, are used, and filling stitches are usually worked before the outline.

Typical stitches

The outline is worked in stem stitch (p. 48), chain stitch (p. 54), or similar stitches, and the shape is then completed with a couched or woven filling stitch. The trellis stitch (p. 109) and honeycomb filling (p. 133) are popular. Knot stitches (pp. 97–100) are also used as filling stitches.

Cutwork

Cutwork first became popular in the sixteenth century. It produces a delicate effect but is, in fact, quite sturdy, since each part of the cut-out design is edged with the buttonhole stitch. The stitching is done first, and then the fabric is cut away. Embroidered bars are used to bridge the larger cut-out areas.

White thread and white fabric were traditionally used for cutwork, which was used on collars, cuffs, and table linen. A number of different forms have developed.

Broderie anglaise

Eyelet and teardrop shapes and scalloped edges are traditional in this technique, which was fashionable in the later-nineteenth century. It developed from Ayrshire embroidery, a form of cutwork that also incorporated surface embroidery and needle-lace filling.

Madeira work

This is a version of broderie anglaise with colored threads. It is named for the island of Madeira, where it originated.

Richelieu work

Picots and buttonhole bars predominate in this technique, which is named for its resemblance to a seventeenth-century Venetian lace.

Renaissance work

The background areas are cut away in this technique, while the motifs are left solid.

The fabric used for cutwork should be

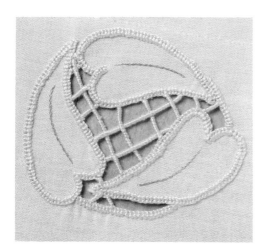

Modern cutwork often uses colored threads to enhance the effect.

firmly woven and not likely to fray. Stranded cotton and silk threads, and pearl cottons are most suitable. When doing cutwork:

1. Mark the design on the fabric, using parallel lines for the buttonhole stitch to keep the stitches the same length. Place a cross in each area to be cut out.

2. Using the same thread as for the buttonhole stitch, outline the design with running stitches, placing them where they will be covered by the buttonhole stitching. Work the buttonhole bars as you come to them (or they may all be worked before the running stitches if preferred).

3. Work the design in the buttonhole stitch, covering the running stitch and making sure that the edges to be cut are solidly covered. Use a double buttonhole stitch if both sides of a line are to be cut.

4. Complete any other embroidery.

5. Using small, very sharp scissors, cut away the unwanted fabric. Work carefully to cut as closely as possible to the edge, but take care not to cut any of the buttonhole stitches.

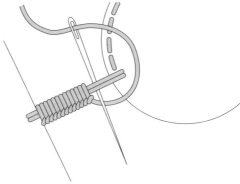

Work buttonhole bars as you come to them.

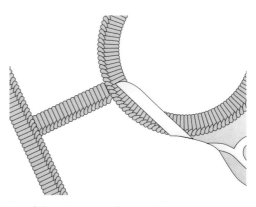

Carefully cut away each area with a cross.

Typical stitches

Buttonhole stitch (p. 81) and its variants and buttonhole bars (p. 84) are used for cutwork. Eyelets (p. 92) may also be included.

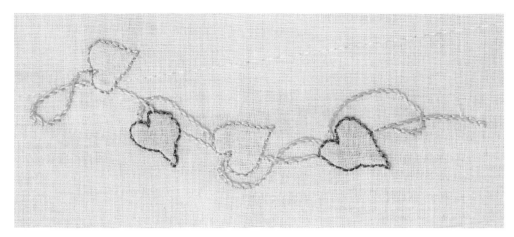

One strand of cotton and a close herringbone stitch were used for this delicate shadow work.

Shadow work

Shadow work was especially popular in the eighteenth century when it was used for white work. White on white is still a popular combination, but shadow work is now also stitched with colored threads. The technique is worked on transparent or semitransparent fabrics, such as voile, organdy, or chiffon. The thread colors should be strong, so they will show through the fabric.

Shadow work originally was worked from the wrong side, using a close herringbone stitch, but it is now sometimes worked from the right side, using a double form of back stitch. Details are added on the right side of the embroidery, using any other surface embroidery stitches that the embroiderer desires.

Each part of a shadow-work design should be narrow and fairly small so that it can be

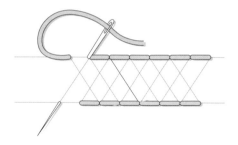

Double back stitch (also known as the shadow stitch).

worked with small stitches. If the stitches are too long, it will be difficult to keep them regular.

When you are preparing to do shadow work embroidery, mark the design in erasable pen on the wrong side of the fabric, remembering that the design will be reversed when the finished embroidery is seen from

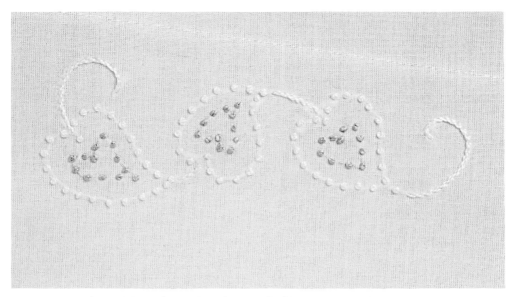

Hearts are a traditional design for candlewicking, worked here in white and green.

the right side. When stitching, use a waste knot to begin, since back stitches will be visible on the finished piece.

Typical stitches

Close herringbone stitch (p. 72) is the basic stitch, while the Holbein stitch (p. 51), stem stitch (p. 48), satin stitch (p. 113), and French knots (p. 98) can be used for details.

Candlewick embroidery

Candlewick embroidery developed in America in the early eighteenth century when settlers used their embroidery skills on the only materials at hand: empty flour bags and the cotton from candle wicks. It is now worked on a range of fabrics, using candlewicking or other cotton threads (stranded or pearl), usually as white-on-white work to reflect the simplicity of its origins. Hearts are often prominent in the designs.

Typical stitches

Colonial knots (p. 99) are characteristic, along with the stem stitch (p. 48), chain stitch (p. 54), and satin stitch (p. 113).

Metallic threads

The use of precious materials in embroidery reached its peak in the later medieval period, from about 1350. Threads of gold and silver were combined with beads and precious stones for a sumptuous effect on clothing for the wealthy and on church vestments.

To make the most conspicuous use of these expensive metallic threads, they were usually applied by couching. This was also the easiest way to apply them, as they can be difficult to use in the same way as more conventional threads: Some will be damaged if they are stitched in and out of the fabric, and others are too stiff. Today gold, silver, copper, and aluminium threads are available in a variety of weights. All are available in true metal or imitation form.

There are a number of different types of metallic thread:

Bullion
is a wire coiled like a tight spring—although it does not spring back if stretched—and hollow in the center. It is normally used in short lengths. If small enough, these can be applied as beads (see pp. 43–5).

Purl
similar to bullion but finer. It is used as a fine, continuous thread.

Twist
consists of two or more wires twisted together into a cord.

Plate
is a flat strip, like a ribbon.

Lurex
is a soft, imitation metal thread that is easier to use than metal threads. It comes in a range of finishes.

Metallic threads can be used to create some very special effects.

Passing thread
also known as Japanese gold or silver, consists of gold- or silver-leaf wrapped around a cotton, flax, or silk core to form a smooth, round thread. The leaf may be real or imitation gold or silver.

Gimp
is similar to passing thread but heavier in weight.

Common techniques

Some of the more common techniques used with metallic threads are:

Cord technique
is used when couching bullion, twists, and purl. The anchoring stitches are slanted to match the twists of the "cord," and pulled tight so that they are not seen.

Couché rentré
is a technique where the anchoring stitches are

brought up and down through the same hole, but on either side of the laid thread, and pulled tightly so that the laid thread kinks down and appears to be forming stitches. The anchoring thread must be strong, and the fabric must have an open weave.

Plunging

is used to secure the ends of the laid thread. Take the laid thread to the back of the fabric, if necessary making a hole with a stiletto or unraveling a thick cord and taking each strand through separately. Then use the anchoring thread to secure it on the back of the work.

Or nué

or Italian shading, is a technique in which gold threads are couched with colored threads to form patterns. The anchoring stitches are grouped, and each part of the design is worked with a separate needle and thread (see pp. 101–3).

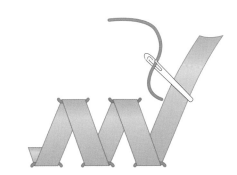

Anchor plate zigzags with a stitch over each fold.

Plate zigzags

can be made by folding the plate strip into zigzags and placing an anchoring stitch at each turn.

String padding

involves sewing lengths of string (which may be dyed to match the metallic thread) to the fabric and covering it with couched threads, using small lengths of bullion or purl or by trailing (see p. 108).

Metallic threads form patterns in or nué.

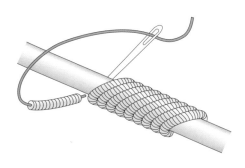

Short lengths of bullion can be applied over string padding.

may also be used. Stitch the padding shapes in place and couch metallic threads over the

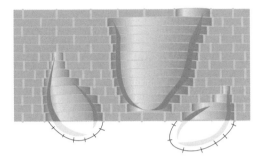

Stitch metallic threads down around the edges of padded shapes.

padding. Stitch at the edge of smaller shapes and work through the padding, if necessary, for larger ones.

When working with metallic threads, always use a frame, so you will have both hands free. A hoop can be used only for small pieces of embroidery because the hoop cannot be fixed over already embroidered areas without damaging the metallic threads.

When couching metallic threads, begin the anchoring thread with a waste knot (p. 22) and complete all the couching. Then plunge the ends of all the laid threads.

Typical stitches

The various couching stitches (pp. 101–12) are generally used.

Quilting and appliqué

Quilting and appliqué are often done by machine today, but traditionally both were done by hand, employing a variety of stitches.

In appliqué, the blind stitch or blanket stitches (pp. 75–9) are sometimes used to attach fabric shapes to the background fabric. Other stitches that can be used include the feather stitch (p. 86) and chain stitch (p. 54). The thread used can match the fabric shape or the background, or can contrast with them to increase the decorative effect. Details are often added with surface embroidery. Heavier stitches, such as the chain stitch (p. 54) and various knot stitches (pp. 97–100) are most effective.

The running stitch (p. 47) is the basic stitch used for hand quilting. Today additional surface embroidery may be added to a quilt, along with appliqué shapes, especially on quilts that are designed to be hung rather than used as bedspreads.

Woven, or raised, stitches were used to create this elegant floral picture.

Raised work

During the seventeenth century raised work, or stump work, became increasingly popular as part of the vogue for embroidered pictures. Small pictures—often showing Biblical or mythological scenes, as well as landscapes, garden scenes, and birds and animals—were embroidered and hung on the wall. The figures and shapes in these pictures were based on "stumps," which were carved from wood in the shapes of heads, arms, legs, and so on, and then covered with embroidery. Silk threads and fabric were

used, and details were added using beads, laces, and metallic threads. In the eighteenth and nineteenth centuries the tradition continued, with a preference for floral arrangements, often worked in wool in a variety of raised stitches.

Modern embroiderers today continue the tradition of raised work, using a variety of techniques to achieve their three-dimensional effects. Raised work requires considerable skill and time to achieve a good result. Use a firm fabric for the background and begin work on the flatter areas. A piece of light cloth can be basted over completed areas to protect them as you work. Some of the most commonly used techniques in raised work are:

Padding

Satin stitch or woven filling stitches can be used over fabric padding to give a raised effect (see "Fabric padding," p. 115). For a higher effect, one side of the fabric can be left open and fiberfill, cotton, or wool can be inserted before the opening is stitched closed.

Fabric slips

A small piece of another fabric (a "slip") can be stitched into the piece. It can be gathered or pleated. Stitch it along one or more edges with tiny stitches and cover free edges with buttonhole stitch or hemming.

Needlepoint slips

A small piece of needlepoint or cross-stitch can be incorporated into raised work. Work the stitches on a piece of canvas or evenweave fabric 2 in. (5 cm) larger all around than the position on the embroidery to be filled. Then pull out threads from this extra fabric, so that there is a fringe all around. Position this slip on the work and take each thread of the fringe to the back of the work, tying them in pairs to anchor the slip. If desired, dab the knots with fabric glue.

Wire

Cut two pieces of fabric to the required shape. With right sides together, stitch around the edge, leaving a small opening. Cut notches in the seam allowance as necessary and turn the shape right side out. Insert wire into the opening and run it around the edge of the shape, leaving about 1 in. (3 cm) at the beginning and end protruding. Stitch the opening closed around the wires and take the wires through the work to the back. Form each end of the wire into a loop and stitch it to the back of the work.

Woven picots are used for the petals of this little flower.

Typical stitches

Any embroidery stitch can be used, especially woven and woven filling stitches (pp. 118–37) and couching stitches (pp. 101–12).

Creating a design

For many embroiderers, part of the pleasure of their work lies in creating the design. Whether you are beginning from scratch or adapting a design from another medium, here are a few guidelines to bear in mind.

First, remember to include a focal point to which the eye will be drawn first. You can emphasize it by using brighter color, larger shapes, leaving space around it, or having lines lead to it.

Second, unless you are using a geometric pattern that depends for its effect on repetition, avoid using shapes that are all the same size and regularly spaced, and avoid equal proportions of color, as these will produce a monotonous result.

Finally, do not go too far the other way and use too many textures (stitches) and colors or too many different shapes, or your design will be too distracting.

COUNTED-THREAD EMBROIDERY

Counted-thread embroidery is worked on evenweave fabrics by counting the threads and working each stitch over a specific number of threads. It is usually worked from a chart (see pp. 19–20). Prepare the fabric (see p. 21) and do a sample piece to decide on the thickness of thread and the size of needle. Counted-thread embroidery is worked with a tapestry needle to avoid splitting the fabric threads.

Mark the center of the fabric and begin working as close to the center as possible. Use a waste knot or waste back stitches to start (see pp. 22–3).

Cross-stitch

Cross-stitch is a very popular form of embroidery, and a good result is not difficult to achieve, as long as all the top stitches lie in the same direction. Always work partial stitches as you come to them and complete all the cross-stitches before adding outlines and other details.

A three-quarter stitch is used when only half the square is to be covered. To make a three-quarter stitch, work the appropriate diagonal and then add a quarter stitch by bringing the needle up in the corner of the square and putting it into the center, either over or under the diagonal, so it matches the other stitches.

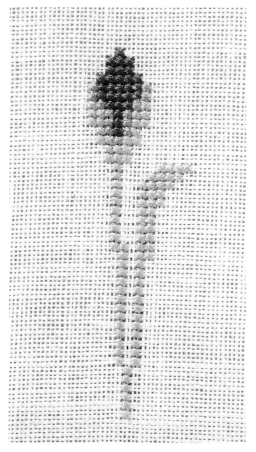

Cross-stitch on evenweave linen is a traditional form of embroidery.

Typical stitches

The cross-stitch (p. 64) and its variations are the basic stitches, while outlines are added in back stitch (p. 48) or Holbein stitch (p. 51). French knots (p. 98) and straight stitch (p. 91) can be used for details.

Versatile cross-stitch can be used for geometric as well as pictorial designs.

Using waste canvas

Waste canvas can be used to work cross-stitch on plainweave fabric. This canvas is made to pull apart when wet, so it can be removed easily when the embroidery is finished.

Cut a piece at least 2 in. (5 cm) larger all around than the design. Baste it to the fabric with the canvas aligned with the straight grain of the fabric and work the cross-stitch design, but use a crewel needle. Once the embroidery is done, remove the basting stitches, dampen the canvas, and remove the canvas threads one by one with tweezers.

You may achieve a better result on lightweight and knit fabrics by stitching interfacing to the back of the fabric. Once the embroidery has been completed the interfacing can be trimmed back close to the edges of the design.

Linen

Linen is one of the oldest textile fibers—examples of linen cloth dating back to 6000 BC have been found in Israel—and until the eighteenth century, linen was the most important cloth. It is soft and strong, with a slightly lustrous appearance. It washes well, is hard-wearing, and can be manufactured so that it is shrinkproof.

This vegetable fiber is produced from the flax plant (*Linum usitatissimum*), which will grow in swampy, mild lowlands almost anywhere in the world. The stalks are cut and laid in water in bundles until the outer fibers have rotted away. The fine, inner fibers are then spun into thread and woven into linen fabric.

Embroidery linen is woven especially for embroidery, usually in natural colors. It has a regular, even weave and can be used for surface and counted-thread work. It is still very popular for working fine cross-stitch pieces. Linen yarn can also be used for embroidery, and it gives a very beautiful result on linen fabric. It does tend to fray in the needle eye, however, and is no longer readily available.

The geometric designs of Assisi work can be very effective, especially when stitched in traditional blue.

Assisi work

Named for the Italian town of Assisi, where it was developed in the medieval period, this technique is generally used for small designs or borders, although it also works well for larger, formal compositions. The main motif is left blank but outlined with dark thread using the Holbein stitch, and the background is filled with cross-stitch. Traditional colors for the background are bright blue or red, and motifs were stylized floral designs, birds, and animals. A border can also be added in the Holbein stitch. White and cream linen were the fabrics used most often.

Typical stitches

The cross-stitch (p. 64) and Holbein stitch (p. 51) are the main stitches used, although details can be added using French knots (p. 98) and small straight stitches (p. 91).

HELPFUL HINT

Never leave the needle in your embroidery. If you do not return to the work for some time, the needle could rust and leave marks on the fabric.

Blackwork

In the sixteenth century blackwork, or Spanish work, spread across Europe from Spain, where it had been introduced by the Moors. It is a monochromatic embroidery, traditionally worked in black thread on white linen, although metallic threads and beads could be added. Clothing, including caps and collars, and pillow covers were the main items decorated in this way.

Strapwork (designs based on interlaced bands) and curving foliage designs were popular, especially worked in the Holbein stitch (p. 51). Variety and tonal effects were achieved by using different weights of thread or varying the density of filling stitches. Today stranded cotton or silks, or pearl threads can be used. Thread colors other than black are now popular, although dark ones still give the most dramatic effect.

Geometric designs can be worked from a chart. For pictorial designs, mark the outline directly onto the fabric. Use filling stitches to shade each area, making each area denser or lighter as appropriate, before adding the outlines.

Typical stitches

The Holbein stitch (p. 51) is the basic stitch, while the back stitch (p. 48), stem stitch (p. 48), chain stitch (p. 54), cross-stitch (p. 64), and satin stitch (p. 113) are also popular.

Monochromatic blackwork is one of the more delicate and restrained forms of embroidery.

HELPFUL HINT

When working with stranded cotton, make sure all strands are threaded with the grain in the same direction. The strands will then sit flatter and look neater.

If stranded thread untwists during stitching, drop the needle so the thread hangs from the work. It will spin back with the correct amount of twist.

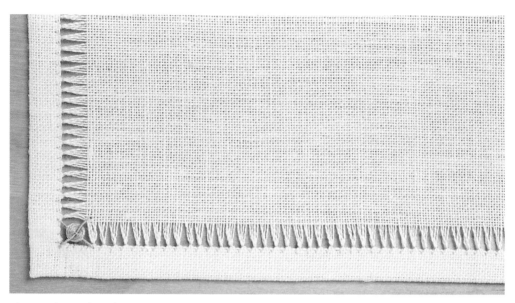

Elegant drawn-thread work is popular for tablecloths and bed linen.

Drawn-thread work

In drawn-thread embroidery, either the horizontal or vertical threads are drawn from the fabric to leave threads in one direction only. They are then stitched together to form patterns (see pp. 143–53) and put strength back into fabric. The technique is used only in narrow bands, mostly for borders on linen, particularly tablecloths. It can be combined with surface embroidery.

Typical stitches

The hem stitch (p. 144) is probably the most common drawn-thread stitch.

Pulled-fabric work

In pulled-fabric work (also known as drawn-fabric work), a thick needle and fine, strong thread are used to pull stitches tight, so that a hole is created in the fabric. The holes can vary in size and are arranged to form patterns. In the finest work, they create a lacelike effect. Eighteenth-century Dresden work was the best example of this technique.

Along with stitches specific to the technique, eyelets are commonly used, as well as blocks of tightly pulled satin stitch to create checkerboard and grid patterns.

Typical stitches

Use the various pulled stitches (pp. 154–7), eyelets (p. 92), and satin stitch (p. 113).

Kloster blocks are used here for the central design and the stepped outline.

Hardanger embroidery

Hardanger embroidery is a form of cutwork stitched on evenweave fabric. It originated in the Hardanger district of Norway and became very popular in the United States at the end of the nineteenth century. Thick cotton or linen thread is used to build up kloster blocks (blocks of satin stitch), and threads are cut away from the squares between them. The remaining threads are overcast or woven using a lighter thread. This technique is traditionally worked in white thread on a white, closely woven (22 or 24 count) evenweave fabric known as Hardanger fabric. Colored threads and other closely woven evenweave fabrics can be used. Hardanger is worked from a chart.

1. Begin by working the kloster blocks, each of which consists of five satin stitches (see below). Work from left to right using a tapestry needle and, in a horizontal or vertical row, leave at least four threads between each block. The blocks can also be worked diagonally (see bottom diagram).

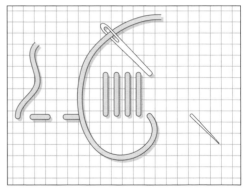

Each kloster block consists of five stitches.

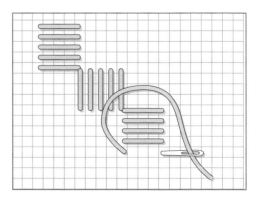

Kloster blocks are also worked diagonally.

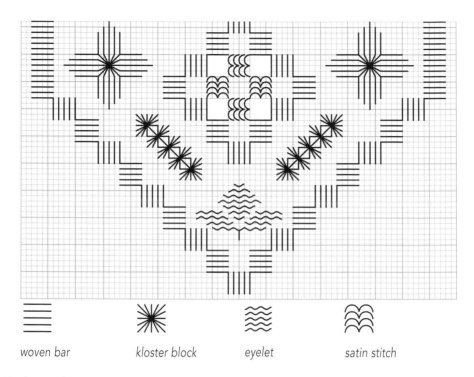

woven bar   kloster block   eyelet   satin stitch

A Hardanger chart.

2. Carefully cut the threads, using small, very sharp scissors. Only threads running between facing kloster blocks can be cut, since the ends of the cut threads must be contained by the satin stitches. Double-check before you cut. Remove the cut threads.

3. The remaining threads can be overcast or woven and filling stitches added in some holes.

Typical stitches

The satin stitch (p. 113), overcast bar (p. 148), woven bar (p. 149), dove's-eye corner (p. 151), and loop stitch (p. 150)—worked into the

kloster blocks instead of the buttonhole stitch—are the most commonly used stitches.

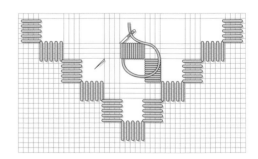

Overcast or weave the remaining threads to create the bars.

BEADWORK

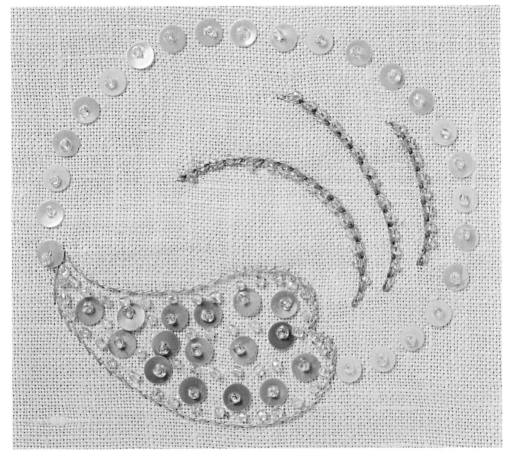

Sequins, like beads, can make effective highlights on embroidery.

Beadwork is a very old form of embroidery. Beads were sewn to fabric for decoration in Palaeolithic times and have been an integral part of many embroidery traditions, adding texture and richness to embroideries as diverse as medieval church vestments, Victorian embroidered pictures, and modern evening bags. They can also be used to create an entire design.

Any small item with a hole in it can be used in beadwork, whether it is a seed pearl, a precious gem, a modern glass bead, or a sequin. The methods of attaching them are the same.

Attaching beads

A single bead can be attached to embroidery very simply. Bring the needle and thread from the back to the front of the fabric where the bead is to sit. Thread the needle through the hole in the bead and then return the needle to the back of the fabric and fasten off.

A number of beads strung onto strong thread can be couched on the surface of the fabric. This is a quicker method if you are covering an area with beads. Anchor the couched string down with a stitch between each bead (see pp. 101–3).

Bead fringe

Each pendant string of beads is attached to the fabric separately. Braid or other trimming is often added to cover the stitches.

Use a strong thread and place a knot in one end. Thread the other end through a needle and then add on the beads. Attach the pendant to the fabric with several firm back stitches.

Attaching sequins

There are a number of ways of attaching sequins to fabric. The thread will be visible to some degree in each case, and should be selected either to match or contrast in a decorative fashion. As the thread will be repeatedly pulled through the sequins, it should be strong and only short lengths should be used. Always work from right to left.

Using one stitch

The stitching thread becomes part of the decoration with this method of securing sequins (see diagram below).

Bring the needle to the front of the fabric at A and thread on a sequin. Insert the needle on the right-hand edge of the sequin at B and bring it out where the next sequin will sit, at C. A–C is the length of one sequin. Continue working back stitches and threading on sequins as required.

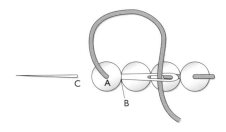

Attaching sequins to fabric with the back stitch.

Using double stitches

In this method of attaching sequins, a line of thread runs across the middle of the sequins (see diagram at right). They are held firmly in place.

Bring the needle up at A and thread on the first sequin. Insert the needle at B, on the right-hand edge of the sequin, and bring it up at C, on the left-hand edge. Finally, insert the needle at A and come up at D. Continue as required.

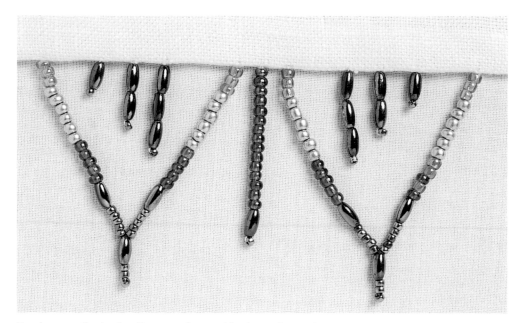

Beads are well suited to fringes and can add color and panache.

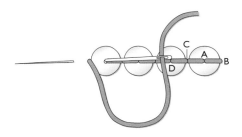

Attaching sequins with double stitches.

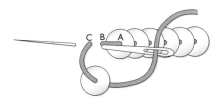

Attaching sequins with hidden stitches.

Using hidden stitches

In this method, the sequins overlap, almost hiding the thread (see diagram above right). Bring the needle to the front of the fabric at A and thread on the first sequin. Insert the needle on the left-hand edge of the sequin at B. Then bring the needle out at C so that B–C is half the length of one sequin. Thread on a sequin and insert the needle at B, bringing it out at D. Continue as required.

Using beads as anchors

Tiny beads may be used to anchor sequins in place. Bring the needle to the front of the fabric and thread on a sequin and then a bead. Insert the needle back through the center of the sequin.

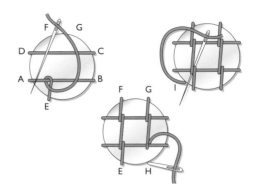

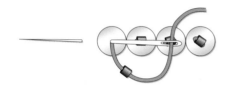

Attaching sequins with beads.

Attaching unpierced items

Mirrors and other flat objects such as coins or metal disks are stitched to fabric using the shisha stitch, also known as the Indian mirror stitch (p. 46).

1. Hold the item in place and bring the needle to the front of the fabric against the lower left-hand edge, at A. Insert it at B to make a horizontal stitch and then make another stitch from C to D.

2. Bring the needle up at E and take it over and under stitch A–B. Then take it over and under stitch C–D and insert it at F. Bring it out at G and repeat the process for C–D and

Stitch a grid over the unpierced item to anchor it to the fabric.

A–B, inserting it at H (see diagram top right).

3. Now bring the needle out at I and take it under the lower left intersection, keeping the thread to the left. Insert the needle back in at I and bring it out at J, with the thread under

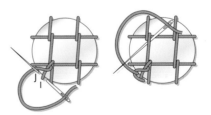

the needle. Then weave around the edges to finish the attachment (see diagram above).

4. Continue working around the item, taking the needle under the grid stitches and the intersections as appropriate.

line stitches

Line stitches include the basic embroidery stitches—running stitch, back stitch, and stem stitch. They can be used on their own and as the basis for woven stitches. They are often combined with other stitches to create original designs.

Line stitches can be worked on plain- or evenweave fabrics, using a crewel needle.

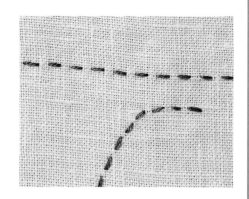

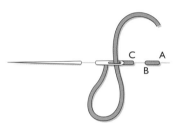

RUNNING *stitch*

This stitch is used for straight or curved lines. The stitches on the front of the fabric should all be the same length, while the spaces between them should be the same length (on evenweave fabric) or shorter (on plainweave fabrics). Work from right to left.

1. Bring the needle to the front of the fabric at A.

2. Insert the needle at B and bring it out at C, making a small stitch.

3. Repeat as necessary.

BACK *stitch*

This stitch is used for straight and curved lines, especially for fine details. Work from right to left.

1. Bring the needle to the front of the fabric at A.

2. Insert the needle to the right of A, at B, and bring it out to the left of A, at C. The distance from A to C should be the same as that from A to B to ensure the stitches are the same length.

3. Continue as required.

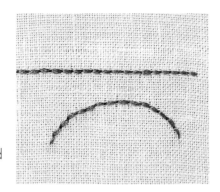

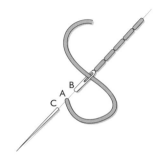

STEM *stitch*

(Crewel stitch, South Kensington stitch)

This stitch is used for straight and curved lines, including flower stems. Work from left to right, keeping the thread below the needle. Stitches should be the same length except on tight curves, where they can be smaller to make a smoother line.

1. Bring the needle to the front of the fabric at A.

2. Insert the needle at B and bring it out at C, halfway between B and A.

3. Now insert the needle at D and bring it out beside B but above the line of stitching. Continue as required.

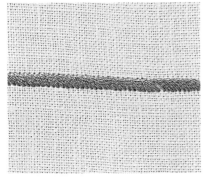

ENCROACHING STEM *stitch*

This stitch is a wider version of the stem stitch, created by angling the needle across the line of the work. The width of the stitch can be altered by adjusting the angle of the needle. Work from left to right.

1. Bring the needle to the front of the fabric at A.

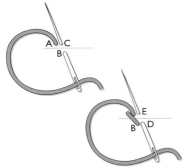

2. Insert the needle below the line to be stitched, at B, and bring it out next to A, at C, keeping the needle angled across the line.

3. Now insert the needle at D and bring it out at E. Continue, keeping the thread below the needle.

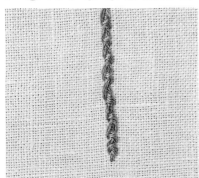

PORTUGUESE KNOTTED STEM *stitch*

This stitch forms a knotted line used for outlining shapes. It is worked from bottom to top.

1. Bring the needle to the front of the fabric at A and insert it at B.

2. Bring the needle out halfway along the left of the stitch, at C, and slide the needle under the stitch from right to left, keeping the thread above the needle. Again slide the needle under the stitch to form a second wrap below the first.

3. Take the needle to the back at D and bring it out at B on the left side of second stem stitch. Then again keeping the thread above the needle, take the needle under both stitches, from right to left. Repeat as before to make a second knot.

4. Continue working in the same way.

OUTLINE *stitch*

This stitch is like the stem stitch, but the thread is kept above the needle. It is used for straight or curved lines. Work from left to right, keeping the stitches the same length.

1. Bring the needle to the front of the fabric at A.

2. Insert the needle at B and bring it out again at A.

3. Now insert the needle at C and bring it out beside B but slightly below the line of stitching. Continue as required.

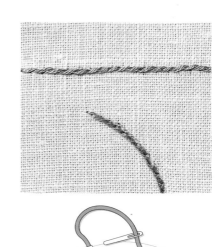

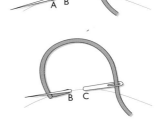

SPLIT *stitch*

(Kensington outline stitch)

This stitch is used for straight and curved outlines and also as a filling stitch. Work from left to right.

1. Bring the needle to the front of the fabric at A.

2. Insert the needle at B. Bring it out at C, splitting the thread.

3. Continue as required.

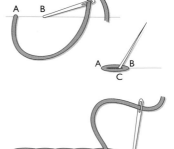

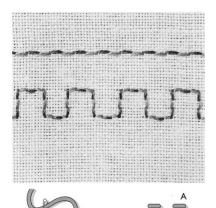

HOLBEIN *stitch*

(Double running stitch)

This stitch looks the same on the front and back if worked carefully. It is used for straight and curved lines. Work from right to left.

1. Bring the needle to the front of the fabric at A and work a line of running stitch (p. 47). Keep the stitches and spaces the same length.

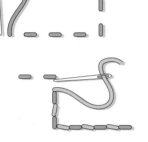

2. Turn the fabric over (or begin again at the right end of the original line) and work another line of running stitch, filling in the spaces in the first line. Bring the needle out below the thread of the first line and insert it above the line, so the stitches of the second line are slightly angled.

DARNING *stitch*

This stitch consists of several rows of running stitch (p. 47) worked closely together. It is used to form brick or block patterns. Work from right to left.

1. Work the first row of running stitch, making sure that the stitches are even in length and longer than the spaces.

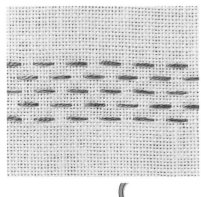

2. Work additional rows of running stitch one or more threads of fabric apart, aligning or staggering the stitches as required.

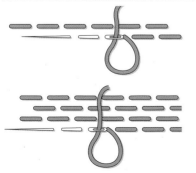

JAPANESE *darning*

This stitch forms meander patterns. Use evenweave fabric and work from right to left.

1. Work two or more rows of running stitch (p. 47), staggering the stitches and ensuring they are even in length and longer than the spaces. Space the rows several threads apart.

2. Join the rows with slanting, vertical stitches by bringing the needle to the front of the fabric at A on the top row and inserting it at B on the second row.

3. Now bring the needle out at C on the second row and insert it at D on the first row.

4. Continue as required.

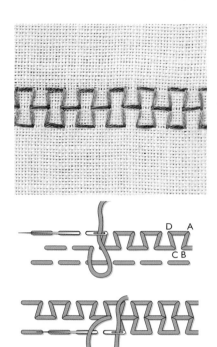

GLOVE *stitch*

(Streatley stitch)

This stitch is used to make zigzags and to join two pieces of fabric. Work on evenweave fabric or mark two parallel lines (see p. 53). Work from left to right.

1. Bring the needle to the front of the fabric at A on the lower line and insert it at B, directly above A.

2. Bring the needle back to the front at A, through the same hole as before, and insert it at C, to the right of B.

3. Bring the needle to the front at D, directly below C, and insert it at C, through the same hole as before.

4. Bring the needle out at D, through the same hole, and in at E, continuing as required.

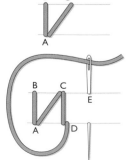

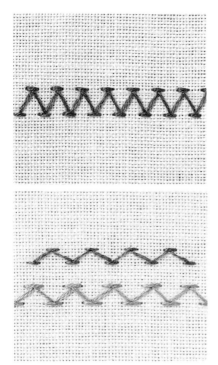

CHEVRON *stitch*

This stitch is used for straight borders. It is worked on evenweave fabric or between two marked parallel lines (see p. 53). Work from left to right.

1. Bring the needle to the front of the fabric at A on the lower line and insert it at B to form a straight stitch.

2. Bring the needle out at C, above and halfway along the stitch.

3. Insert the needle at D on the upper line and bring it out at E, then in at F and out at D.

4. On the lower line, insert the needle at G, bring it out at H, and continue as required.

HELPFUL HINT
marking guidelines

When working some stitches on plainweave fabric, it is necessary to mark guidelines or grids to ensure a neat, regular result. Mark the lines with a water-erasable pen or sharp chalk pencil and a ruler—a metal one will give the neatest line. If you require more than one line, measure carefully at each end to ensure they are parallel.

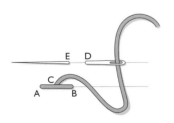

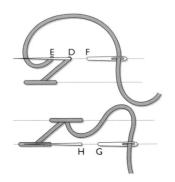

chain stitches

Chain stitch is a basic embroidery stitch and has a number of variations. They are used to create curved and straight lines and, in repeated rows, as filling. The loops should all be the same size and not pulled so tightly that they lose their rounded shape.

Chain stitches are worked on plainweave or evenweave fabrics using a crewel needle.

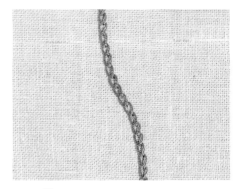

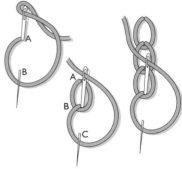

CHAIN *stitch*

This stitch is used to make broad straight and curved lines. Work from top to bottom.

1. Bring the needle to the front of the fabric at A.

2. Insert the needle again at A, bringing it out at B. Keep the thread under the needle as you pull the thread through.

3. Insert the needle at B and bring it out at C, continuing as required.

4. To finish, make a small stitch over the last loop.

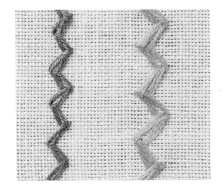

ZIGZAG CHAIN *stitch*

This stitch is used for broad zigzag lines. On evenweave fabric, work over a consistent number of threads; on plainweave fabric, mark two parallel lines (see p. 53). Work from top to bottom.

1. Bring the needle to the front of the fabric at A.

2. Insert the needle again at A, bringing it out to the right at B. Keep the thread under the needle.

3. Insert the needle at B, bringing it out to the left at C, and continue as required.

4. To finish, make a small stitch over the last loop.

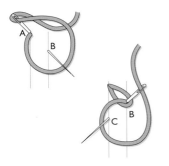

OPEN CHAIN *stitch*

(Square chain stitch, Roman chain stitch)

This stitch gives a ladderlike effect. On evenweave fabric, work over a consistent number of threads; on plainweave fabric, mark two parallel lines (see p. 53). Work from top to bottom.

1. Bring the needle to the front of the fabric at A.

2. Insert the needle at B and bring it out at C, with the thread under the needle. Leave the thread slightly loose.

3. Insert the needle at D and bring it out for the next stitch, continuing as required.

4. Hold the last loop in place by making two small stitches, one at each corner of the loop.

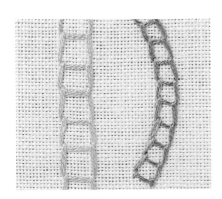

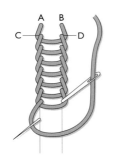

HEAVY CHAIN *stitch*

(Braid stitch)

1. Working from the top, bring the needle to the front of the fabric at A and insert it at B to make a small stitch.

2. Bring the needle out at C and take it under the small stitch from right to left, slipping it along the top of the fabric. Then insert it at C.

3. Now bring the needle out at D, again take it under the small stitch in the same way and insert it at D.

4. Bring the needle out at E and now take it under both the chain stitches from right to left before inserting it at E.

5. Continue as required, always taking the needle under both the previous two stitches at the same time.

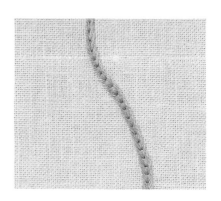

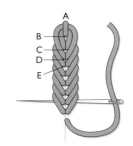

DOUBLE CHAIN *stitch*

Work this stitch on evenweave fabric or mark two parallel lines (see p. 53). Work from top to bottom, keeping the thread under the needle.

1. Bring the needle to the front of the fabric at A.

2. Insert the needle at B, to the right and above A. Bring it out at C, the same distance below A as B was above.

3. Insert the needle at A and bring it out at D so that the stitch is the same length as B–C.

4. Now insert the needle at C and bring it out at E, working in the same way.

5. Continue as required, finishing with a small stitch over the last loop.

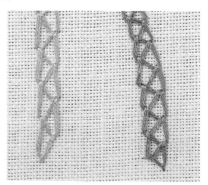

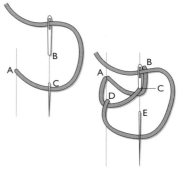

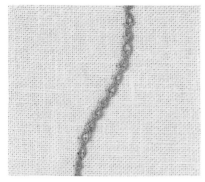

TWISTED CHAIN *stitch*

This stitch is used for textured straight and curved lines. Work from top to bottom.

1. Bring the needle to the front of the fabric at A.

2. Insert the needle at B to the left of A on the line and bring it out at C, to the right of the line, with the thread passing over and then under the needle. Keep the stitches small for the neatest result.

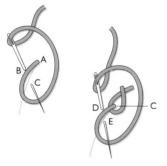

3. Insert the needle at D to the left of previous loop and bring it out at E, working in the same way.

4. Continue as required, finishing with a small stitch over the last loop.

CABLE CHAIN *stitch*

This stitch is used for straight or curved lines. The linking stitches can be short or long, as required. Work from top to bottom.

1. Bring the needle to the front of the fabric at A.

2. Insert the needle at A, bringing it out below A, at B. Keep the thread under the needle.

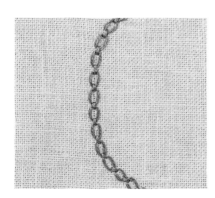

3. Twist the thread around the needle to the right and hold it with your thumb.

4. Insert the needle at C to form the link and bring it out at D, with the thread under the needle.

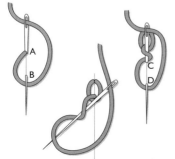

5. Continue as required, finishing with a small stitch over the last loop.

FEATHERED CHAIN *stitch*

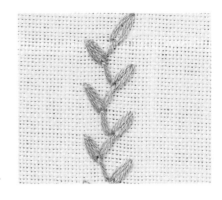

This stitch forms a neat border. On evenweave fabric, work over a consistent number of threads; on plainweave fabric, mark two parallel lines (see p. 53). Work from top to bottom.

1. Bring the needle to the front of the fabric on the right-hand line at A.

2. Insert the needle at A and bring it out at B, with the thread under the needle.

3. Insert the needle at C so that A–B–C form a straight line and bring it out at D, which is on the left-hand line and level with B (see diagram 1).

4. Insert the needle at D and bring it out at C, keeping the thread under the needle (see diagram 2).

5. Insert the needle at E so that D–C–E form a straight line and bring it out at F, which is on the right-hand line and level with C (see diagram 3).

6. Now insert the needle in at F and bring it out at E to make the next chain stitch (see diagram 4).

7. Continue as required, finishing with a small stitch over the last chain.

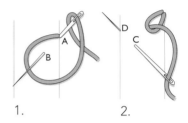

1.   2.

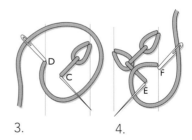

3.   4.

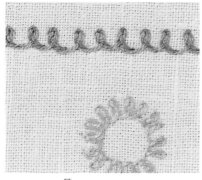

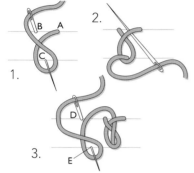

ROSETTE CHAIN *stitch*

(Bead edging)

This stitch is used for edgings and circles. Flower motifs can be made from several concentric rings of stitches. On evenweave fabric, work over a consistent number of threads; on plainweave fabric, mark two parallel lines (see p. 53). Work from right to left.

1. Bring the needle to the front of the fabric on the upper line at A.

2. Form the thread into a twisted loop over the lower line, to the left of A, and hold it down with your thumb.

3. Insert the needle at B and bring it out at C, inside the loop and on the lower line, slightly to the right of B (see diagram 1).

4. Take the needle under the first part of the stitch, slipping it along the top of the fabric (see diagram 2).

5. Form a twisted loop and stitch from D to E as before, continuing as required (see diagram 3).

HELPFUL HINT

When stitching in a circle, don't angle the needle backward but keep it vertical to the inner line.

MAGIC CHAIN *stitch*

(Two-color chain stitch, alternating chain stitch, checkered chain stitch)

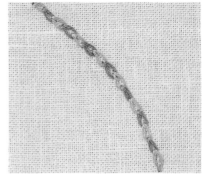

This stitch is worked with two threads of different colors. One or more loops can be worked in each color before changing. Work from top to bottom.

1. Thread both threads onto the needle. Bring the needle to the front of the fabric at A.

2. Insert the needle at A and bring it out at B, with the darker thread under the needle and the lighter over it.

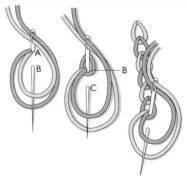

3. Insert the needle at B and bring it out at C, with the lighter thread under the needle and the darker over it.

4. Continue as required and finish with a small stitch over the last chain.

BRAID *stitch*

For the best results, use small stitches and a nonstranded thread. On evenweave fabric, work over a consistent number of threads; on plainweave fabric, mark two parallel lines (see p. 53). Work from right to left.

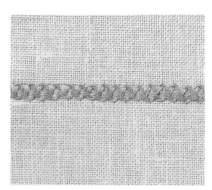

1. Bring the thread to the front of the fabric on the lower line at A.

2. Form a loop with the thread crossing behind itself and hold it with your thumb. Insert the needle through the loop at B and bring it out at C. Do not pull it through.

3. Take the thread under the needle from right to left, pull the thread firmly around the needle, and then pull the needle through and downward.

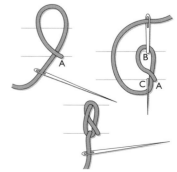

4. Form a loop as in step 1 and continue as required.

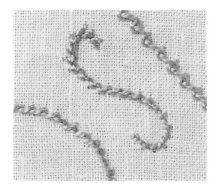

SCROLL *stitch*

(Single knotted-line stitch)

This stitch is used for straight and curved borders. For the best results, use a nonstranded thread. Work from left to right.

1. Bring the thread to the front of the fabric at A.

2. Make a loop with the thread in a clockwise direction, to the right of A, and hold it with your thumb.

3. Insert the needle at B and bring it out at C, with the loop under the needle, and pull the thread through firmly.

4. Continue as required and finish with a small stitch over the last chain.

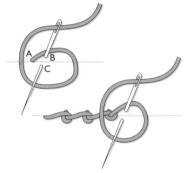

CORAL *stitch*

(Knotted stitch, German knot stitch, beaded stitch, snail trail)

This stitch gives a beaded effect to a line. Space the knots as desired, staggering them when using rows for filling. For the best results, use a nonstranded thread. Work from right to left or from top to bottom.

1. Bring the thread to the front of the fabric at the end of the line at A.

2. Lay the thread along the line and hold it down with your thumb.

3. Make a small vertical stitch across the thread from B to C, with the thread under the needle. Continue as required and finish with a small stitch over the last chain.

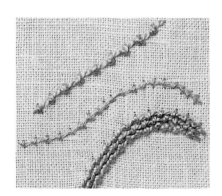

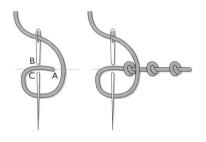

SPANISH CORAL *stitch*

(Crested chain stitch)

This stitch is used for broad, textured lines. For the best results use a nonstranded thread. The stitch consists of a row of chain stitches linked to an upper row of coral stitches by vertical threads. On evenweave fabric, work over a consistent number of threads; on plainweave fabric, mark two parallel lines (see p. 53). The lines can be spaced close together or farther apart as required. Work from right to left.

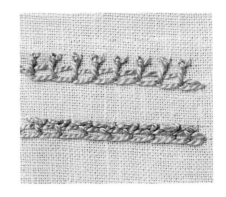

1. Bring the needle to the front of the fabric on the lower line at A.

2. Insert the needle at A and bring it out at B, taking the thread under the needle from top to bottom (see diagram 1).

3. Insert the needle at C on the upper line and bring it out at D, with the thread going up between C and D and then coming down under the needle (see diagram 2).

4. Without piercing the fabric, take the needle under the vertical thread from right to left (see diagram 3).

5. Then insert the needle at B and bring it out at E, again keeping the thread under the needle (see diagram 4).

6. Continue as required, finishing with a small stitch over the last loop (see diagram 5).

1.

2.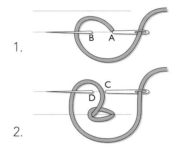

3.

4.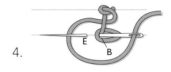

5.

ROPE *stitch*

This stitch is used for raised straight or curved lines. Rows can be worked closely together to fill a shape. For the best results, use fairly long stitches and a nonstranded thread. Work from top to bottom.

1. Bring the needle to the front of the fabric at A.

2. Loop the thread over the line and insert the needle outside the loop at B. Bring it out inside the loop at C. Pull through firmly. Both B and C are on the line.

3. Again loop the thread over the line and put the needle in at D, close to the top of the previous stitch. Bring it out on the line at E and pull the thread through firmly.

4. Continue as required, finishing with a small stitch over the last chain.

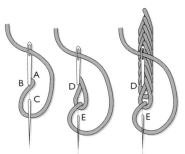

PALESTRINA *stitch*

(Double knot stitch, tied coral stitch, Smyrna stitch, old English stitch, single Danish knot)

Work from left to right or top to bottom, with the knots evenly spaced and close together.

1. Bring the needle to the front of the fabric at A. Insert the needle above the line at B and bring it out below the line at C.

2. Take the needle under the stitch from top to bottom without catching the fabric. Pull through gently.

3. Bring the needle around and again take it under the same stitch, to the right of the last pass, keeping the thread below the needle. Pull the thread through gently. Continue as required.

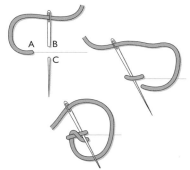

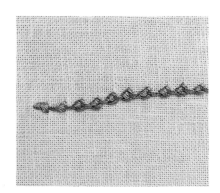

crossed stitches

Crossed stitches include cross-stitch and herringbone stitch and their variations. Cross-stitch, in particular, is very popular, and a good result is easy to achieve as long as the stitches are always worked in the same direction.

Crossed stitches are usually worked on evenweave fabrics using a crewel needle, although a tapestry needle can be used for cross-stitch worked on coarser weaves. Be careful not to split the thread of the first stitches when you are working on the second pass along each row.

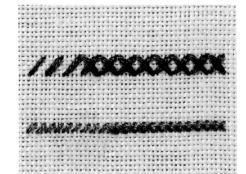

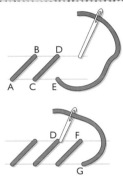

CROSS-*stitch*

(Sampler stitch)

This stitch can be worked in any direction, but the top threads of the stitches should all lie in the same direction. Stitches should all be the same length and slope.

1. Bring the needle to the front of the fabric at A.

2. Insert the needle at B and bring it out at C, then in at D, out at E, and in at F, continuing to complete the row.

3. To return, use the same holes in the fabric, bringing the needle out at G and in at D. Continue to the end of the row.

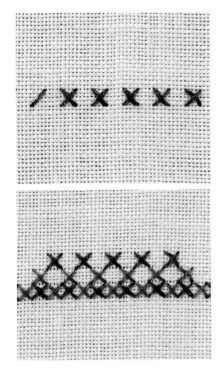

DOUBLE-SIDED CROSS-*stitch*

(Brave brede stitch)

This stitch is the same on both sides and is used on fine fabrics where threads on the back would show through. Every second stitch is worked first, and then the intervening stitches are filled in. Extra half-diagonals are worked to change direction, so a fine thread will give the best result. Mark parallel lines if not using evenweave fabric (see p. 53).

1. Bring the needle to the front of the fabric at A.

2. Working on every second stitch, insert the needle at B and bring it out at C, continuing to the end of the row.

3. Bring the needle out at D, under the center of the last stitch, insert it at E, and then bring it out at D and put it in at F to make two half diagonals.

4. Now bring the needle out at E and insert it at F to complete the turn (see diagram 1).

5. Work back to complete the crosses, bringing the needle out at G and inserting it at H and continuing to the end of the row (see diagram 2).

6. To fill in the spaces, bring the needle out at I and put it in at H. Continue working diagonals across each space. At the end of the row, bring the needle out at E and insert it at D, under the complete diagonal.

7. Bring the needle out at J and continue to the end of the row to complete the crosses (see diagram 3).

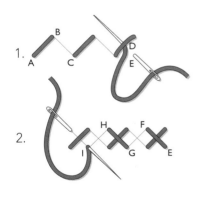

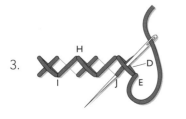

MARKING
CROSS-*stitch*

This stitch has a row of crosses on the front (see top photograph) and a row of squares on the back (see lower photograph). Mark parallel lines if not using evenweave fabric (see p. 53). Work from left to right or top to bottom.

1. Knot the end of the thread and insert the needle about 1 in. (3 cm) from the beginning of the row, leaving the knot on the front of the fabric.

2. Bring the needle to the front of the fabric at A and insert it at B, then bring it out at C and insert it at D to form a cross-stitch.

3. Now bring the needle out at B. Insert it at A and bring it out at C. (There are now three sides of a square on the back.)

4. Insert the needle at E and bring it out at F to begin the second cross, then insert it at A and bring it out at E. Now insert the needle at C and bring it out at F.

5. Continue as required to the end of the row.

6. Cut the waste knot and use the thread to complete the first square. Run the excess thread behind the stitches.

front

back

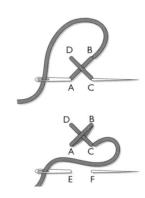

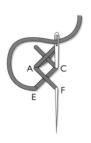

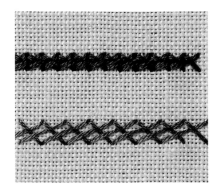

LONG-ARMED
CROSS-*stitch*

*(Long-legged cross-stitch, braided Slav stitch,
Portuguese stitch, and twist stitch)*

This stitch is usually worked on evenweave fabric, and all the top stitches should slant in the same direction. Mark parallel lines if not using evenweave fabric (see p. 53). Work from left to right.

1. Bring the needle to the front of the fabric at A.

2. Insert the needle at B and bring it out at C, on the same line as B and halfway between A and B.

3. Now insert the needle at D, on the lower line and below B, and bring it out at E, on the lower line and below C. Continue as required.

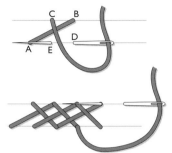

TIED CROSS-*stitch*

This stitch is used for large crosses, as the tie stitch holds the arms in place. It can be stitched singly, in rows, or as filling. It is usually worked on evenweave fabric and should be worked over an even number of threads so the tie stitch will be in the center.

1. Bring the needle to the front of the fabric at A and insert it at B.

2. Bring the needle out at C and insert it at D to form a cross-stitch.

3. Bring the needle to the front again at E and insert it at F, tying down the center of the cross-stitch.

4. To begin the next cross-stitch, bring the needle out at C. Continue as required.

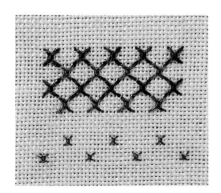

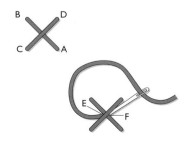

UPRIGHT CROSS-*stitch*

(St. George cross-stitch)

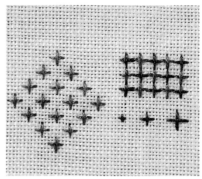

This stitch may be used singly, in rows, or as filling. The top threads should all be vertical. Work from right to left.

1. Bring the needle to the front of the fabric at A and insert it at B. Continue making running stitches to the end of the row.

2. At the end of the row, bring the needle to the front at C and insert it at D, making a vertical stitch across the last running stitch.

3. Then bring the needle out at E and continue making vertical stitches to the end of the row.

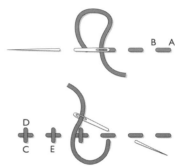

DOUBLE CROSS-*stitch*

(Star stitch, devil stitch)

This stitch can be worked singly or in a row. Work rows on evenweave fabric, or mark three parallel lines (see p. 53). Work from right to left.

1. Bring the needle to the front of the fabric at A.

2. Insert the needle at B, then bring it out at C and insert it at D to complete a cross-stitch.

3. Bring the needle out at E and put it in at F, and then bring it out at G and insert it at H to add an upright cross-stitch on top.

4. Bring the needle up at C and continue along the row as required.

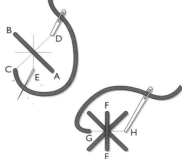

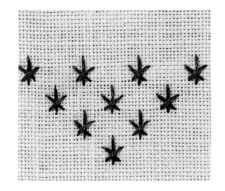

ERMINE *stitch*

(Ermine filling stitch)

This stitch is used singly or in rows. For rows, work over a consistent number of threads on evenweave fabric; on plainweave fabric, mark two parallel lines (see p. 53).

1. Bring the needle to the front of the fabric at A.

2. Insert the needle at B and bring it out at C, which should be lower than B by about a third of the distance from A to B.

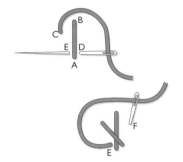

3. Now insert the needle at D and bring it out at E, both at the same level and slightly higher than A.

4. Finally, insert the needle in at F, level with C.

CROSS-AND-STRAIGHT *stitch*

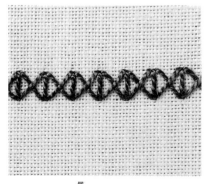

This stitch is a combination of cross-stitch and straight stitch, used to make a band or edging. If preferred, a row of cross-stitch can be stitched and then the straight stitches added. On evenweave fabrics, work over a consistent number of threads; on plainweave fabrics, mark two parallel lines (see p. 53). Work from right to left.

1. Bring the needle to the front of the fabric on the lower line, at A.

2. Insert the needle at B and bring it out directly below at C. Then insert it at D, directly above A, and bring it out at C.

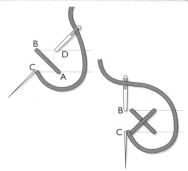

3. Insert the needle at B and bring it out at C to complete the first stitch. Continue as required.

ZIGZAG *stitch*

This stitch is used for borders or filling. Work on evenweave fabric or mark two parallel lines for each line of stitches (see p. 53). Work from right to left.

1. Bring the needle to the front of the fabric at A. Insert it at B and bring it out again at A.

2. Now insert the needle at C, bring it out at D and then again in at C, and out at D. Continue to the end of the row, ending with a vertical stitch.

3. To work back along the row, bring the needle to the front at E. Then insert it at F and bring it out at E.

4. Insert the needle at G and bring it to the front at H, continuing to the end of the row.

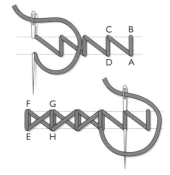

FISHBONE *stitch*

This stitch is used for solid shapes, such as borders, leaves, and wings. Work from top to bottom (or tip to base).

1. Mark the outline and central line of the required shape on the fabric with a water-soluble pen.

2. Bring the needle to the front of the fabric at A on the center line. Insert it at B and bring it out at C, on the edge of the shape.

3. Now insert the needle at D, slightly overlapping the first stitch, and bring it out at E on opposite edge of the shape to C.

4. Insert the needle at F, slightly overlapping the last stitch, and bring it out at G to complete the first fishbone stitch.

5. Continue as required, working on alternate sides of the shape.

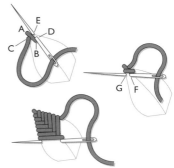

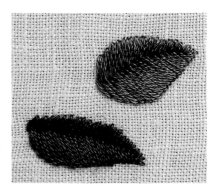

RAISED FISHBONE
stitch

(Overlapping herringbone stitch)

This stitch is used for small raised areas, such as leaves. Outline the shape on the fabric and mark the center.

1. Bring the needle to the front of the fabric at A, at the top of the shape.

2. Insert the needle at the center, at B, and bring it out at C, on the edge of the shape and level with B.

3. Now insert the needle at D, which is on the edge of the shape and very slightly to the right of A, and bring it out at E, very slightly to the left of A.

4. Insert the needle at F, level with C, and bring it out at G, on the edge of the shape and very slightly below C.

5. Insert the needle on the shape, just below D, and bring it out just below E.

6. Now insert the needle at H, just below F, and continue until the shape is covered.

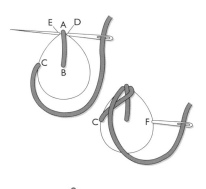

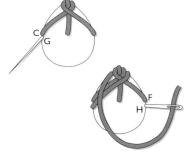

HERRINGBONE *stitch*

(Braided stitch, catch stitch, Russian cross-stitch)

This stitch is used for decorative borders. On evenweave fabric, work over a consistent number of threads; on plainweave fabric, mark two parallel lines for each line of stitches (see p. 53). For the best results, make parallel stitches of equal length. Work from left to right.

1. Bring the needle to the front of the fabric on the lower line at A.

2. Insert the needle on the upper line at B and bring it out at C, so both points are to the right of A (see diagram 1).

3. Insert the needle on the lower line at D, to the right of B, and bring it out at E, to the left of D on the lower line. Continue as required (see diagram 2).

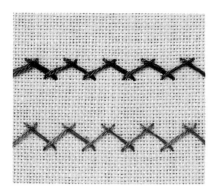

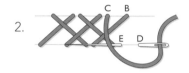

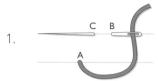

CLOSED HERRINGBONE *stitch*

This stitch is used for straight or curving borders. Work on evenweave fabric or mark two parallel lines (see p. 53). Work from left to right.

1. Bring the needle to the front of the fabric on the upper line at A.

2. Insert the needle at B, bring it out at C, and insert it at D to form a cross.

3. Bring the needle out at E, just to the right of A, and insert it at F, just to the right of B (see diagram 1).

4. Now bring it to the front at G and insert it at H, just to the right of C and D, respectively.

5. Continue, keeping the stitches evenly spaced.

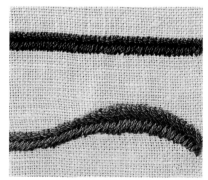

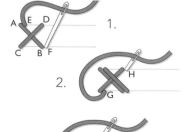

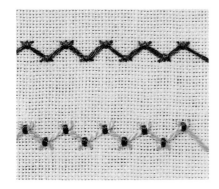

TIED HERRINGBONE
stitch

This stitch is used for zigzag lines, or rows can be worked closely together as filling. Work on evenweave fabric or mark two parallel lines for each line of stitches (see p. 53). Work from left to right.

1. Bring the needle to the front of the fabric on the lower line and work a row of herringbone stitch (see diagram 1).

2. Now work back along the row from right to left. Bring the needle to the front at A.

3. Insert the needle at B to form the first tie and bring it out at C, below the next cross.

4. Insert the needle at D and bring it out at E. Continue to the end of the row (see diagram 2).

1.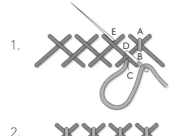

2.

RAISED HERRINGBONE *stitch*

This stitch is used for raised leaf and petal shapes, either singly or in groups. It can be worked with the stitches close together or spaced out for an open effect. Outline the shape on the fabric.

1. Bring the needle to the front of the fabric at A, at the blunt end of the shape.

2. Insert the needle at B to make a small vertical stitch and bring it out at C (see diagram 1).

3. Slide the needle under the vertical stitch, not catching the fabric, from right to left (see diagram 2).

4. Insert the needle at D and bring it out at E. Continue as required.

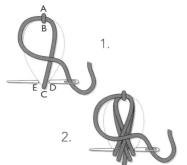

1.

2.

DOUBLE HERRINGBONE *stitch*

(Indian herringbone stitch)

This stitch is often worked in two colors. Work on evenweave fabric or mark two parallel lines for each line of stitches (see p. 53). Work from left to right.

1. Bring the needle to the front of the fabric at A, on the lower line.

2. Insert the needle at B on the upper line, to the right of A, so the stitches will be spaced fairly widely, and bring it out at C. Then take the needle under the stitch from left to right, slipping it along the top of the fabric (see diagram 1).

3. Now insert the needle at D on the lower line and bring it out at E. Continue to the end of the row, taking the needle under the stitch when coming down from the upper line but not when going up from the lower line (see diagram 2).

4. Working with the second color, bring the needle to the front of the fabric on the upper line at F, directly above the beginning of the first row.

5. Insert the needle at G on the lower line and bring it out at H (see diagram 3).

6. Take the needle under the stitch of the first row and then insert it at I on the upper line and bring it out at J (see diagram 4).

7. Take the needle under the stitch just completed and continue to the end of the row, taking the needle under the stitch just completed when coming down from the upper row and under the original row of herringbone

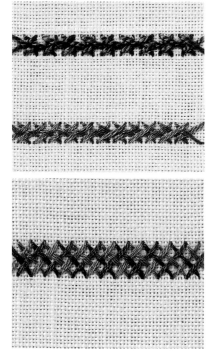

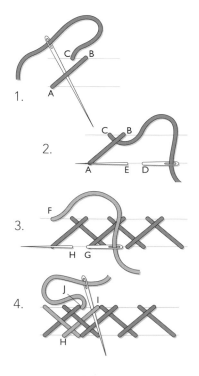

blanket
stitches

Blanket stitches have developed
from the traditional stitch used
to edge blankets. The horizontal
part of the stitch gives a neat
finish to a raw fabric edge and
prevents it from fraying. They
are also used for appliqué and,
when worked closely together,
for edging buttonholes.
Decorative versions have
developed for use as bands and
borders.

These stitches are suitable for
plainweave or evenweave fabrics
and are worked with a crewel
needle.

BLANKET *stitch*

Space the verticals as required. If they are
touching, this is known as a buttonhole
stitch (p. 81). Work on evenweave fabric
or mark two parallel lines (see p. 53).
Work from left to right, keeping the loops
on the edge the same size.

1. Bring the needle to the front of the
fabric at A (on the edge if the stitch is
used as edging).

2. Insert the needle at B and bring it out
at C (on the edge), with the thread under
the needle.

3. Insert the needle at D and continue. To
finish, make a small stitch at E on wrong side
of fabric.

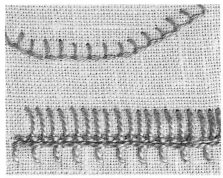

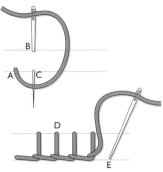

LONG-AND-SHORT BLANKET *stitch*

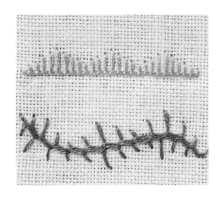

This stitch is used as a decorative edging for straight lines, scallops, or zigzags. Work from left to right.

1. Bring the needle to the front of the fabric, on the edge if the stitch is used as edging.

2. Work the blanket stitch (p. 75) along the edge, varying the height of the verticals to form a consistent pattern.

3. To finish off, make a small stitch on the edge or lower line.

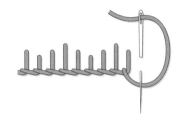

DOUBLE BLANKET *stitch*

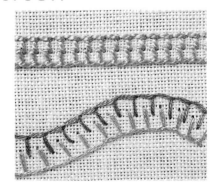

This stitch is used for straight or curved lines and can be worked in two colors. On evenweave fabrics, work over a consistent number of threads; on plainweave fabrics, mark two parallel lines (see p. 53). Work from left to right.

1. Bring the needle to the front of the fabric.

2. Work a row of blanket stitch with the verticals all the same length (see p. 75).

3. Turn the fabric upside down and bring the needle to the front of the fabric on the lower line.

4. Work a second row of blanket stitch, placing each vertical in the center of the verticals of the previous row. Make these stitches the same length and height as those of the previous row and ensure the verticals overlap. To finish, make a small stitch on the edge or lower line.

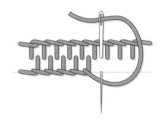

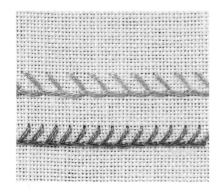

SLOPING BLANKET
stitch

This stitch is used for straight and curved edging. The stitches can be sloped left or right. On evenweave fabrics, work over a consistent number of threads; on plainweave, mark two parallel lines (see p. 53). Work from left to right.

1. Bring the needle to the front of the fabric at A (on the edge if the work is to serve as an edging).

2. Insert the needle at B and bring it out at C, very close to A, with the thread under the needle. Insert the needle at D and, with the thread under the needle, emerge at E, directly below B.

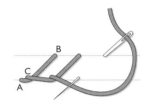

3. Continue as required, sloping the vertical stitches, finishing with a small stitch on the edge or lower line.

CROSSED SLOPING BLANKET *stitch*

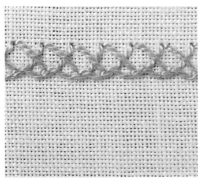

This stitch is used for straight and curved edging. On evenweave fabrics, work over a consistent number of threads; on plainweave fabrics, mark two parallel lines for each line of stitches (see p. 53). Work from left to right.

1. Bring the needle to the front of the fabric at A (on the edge if the work is forming edging).

2. Insert the needle at B and bring it out at C, with the thread looped under the needle.

3. Now insert the needle at D, above A, and bring it out at E, below B, to complete a crossed stitch.

4. Insert the needle at F and bring it out at G. Continue as required, finishing with a small stitch on the edge or lower line.

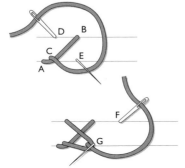

CLOSED BLANKET
stitch

(Closed buttonhole stitch)

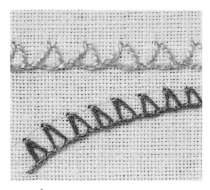

Work this stitch on evenweave fabric or mark two parallel lines for each line of stitches (see p. 53). Work from left to right, keeping each sloping stitch the same length and slope.

1. Bring the needle to the front of the fabric at A (on the edge if the work is forming an edging).

2. Insert the needle at B and bring it out at C, with the thread below the needle.

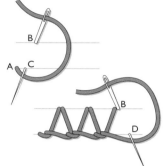

3. Now insert the needle at B and bring it out at D, again with the thread under the needle. Continue as required, finishing with a small stitch on the edge or lower line.

OVERLAPPING BLANKET *stitch*

(Encroaching blanket stitch)

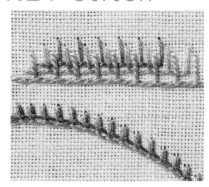

This stitch may be worked in two colors. Use evenweave fabric or mark three parallel lines for each line of stitches (see p. 53). Work from left to right.

1. Bring the needle to the front of the fabric (on the edge if the work is forming edging). Stitch a row of blanket stitch (p. 75), keeping the spaces regular. Finish with a small stitch on the edge or lower line.

2. Now stitch a second row of blanket stitch, with the base close below that of the first row and the verticals consistently spaced between those of the first row (either just to the left, just to the right or in the center).

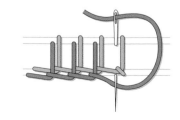

3. Finish with a small stitch on the edge or lower line.

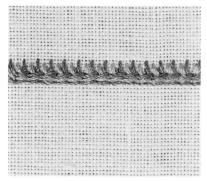

LOOPED BLANKET
stitch

Work this stitch on evenweave fabric or mark two parallel lines for each line of stitches (see p. 53). Work from left to right.

1. Bring the needle to the front of the fabric at A, on the upper line.

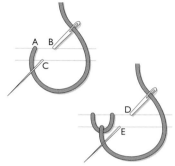

2. Insert the needle at B on the upper line and bring it out at C, on the lower line, with the thread under the needle.

3. Hold the thread to the left with your thumb. Insert the needle at D on the upper line and bring it out at E on the lower one, again with the thread under the needle.

4. Work additional rows in other colors, as desired.

BLANKET PINWHEEL

(Blanket-stitch pinwheel, buttonhole pinwheel)

This stitch is used mainly for flowers.

1. Mark the circle and center on the fabric. Bring the needle to the front of the fabric at A on the outer edge of the circle.

2. Insert the needle at the center and bring it out on the edge, with the thread under the needle. Continue working toward the right (counterclockwise), spacing the stitches evenly around the edge.

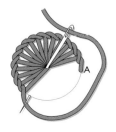

3. To finish, bring the needle out at the center and insert it at A, in the same hole as before, with the thread under the needle. To finish, do a few back stitches on wrong side of work.

KNOTTED BLANKET
stitch

(Knotted buttonhole stitch)

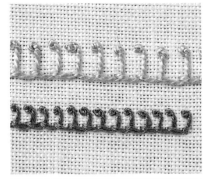

This stitch is used for edging, curved lines, and circles. It is worked the same way as the blanket stitch but with a knot at the top of each vertical. The same method can be used to add knots to the sloping blanket stitch (p. 77) or up-and-down blanket stitch (p. 81). On evenweave fabrics, work over a consistent number of threads; on plainweave fabrics, mark parallel lines for each line of stitches (see p. 53). Work from left to right.

1. Bring the needle to the front of the fabric on the lower line at A.

2. Wind the thread around your thumb. Take the needle through the loop from bottom to top and slip the loop onto the needle.

3. Insert the needle at B on the upper line and bring it out at C, below B on the lower line. Keep the loop on the needle and the thread under the tip of the needle.

4. Holding the knot with your thumb, pull the thread through.

5. Continue as required, finishing with a small stitch on the lower line.

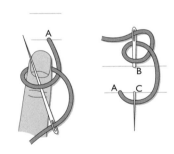

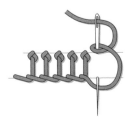

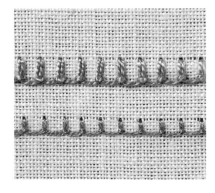

UP-AND-DOWN BLANKET *stitch*

(Up-and-down buttonhole stitch)

Work this stitch on evenweave fabric or mark parallel lines for each line of stitches (see p. 53). Work from left to right.

1. Bring the needle to the front of the fabric on the lower line (or on the edge of the fabric) at A.

2. Insert the needle at B on the upper line and bring it out at C, keeping the thread under the needle.

3. Take the thread to the left of the needle and insert the needle at D. Bring it up on the upper line at E, taking the thread behind the point of the needle. Continue as required.

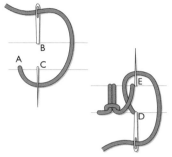

BUTTONHOLE *stitch*

This stitch is used primarily for edgings and buttonholes, but it can also make a decorative border. The verticals are close together with no fabric showing between them. (If fabric shows, the stitch is known as the blanket stitch, p. 75.) Work from left to right, keeping the loops on the edge the same size.

1. Bring the needle to the front of the fabric at A, which is on the edge if the stitch is used for a buttonhole.

2. Insert the needle at B and bring it out at C (on the edge), with the thread under the needle.

3. Continue as required. To finish off, make a small stitch on the edge.

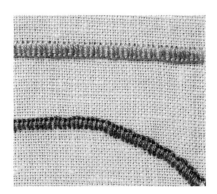

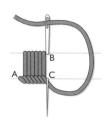

TAILOR'S BUTTONHOLE *stitch*

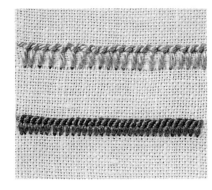

This true buttonhole stitch makes a firm edging or buttonhole. The verticals are usually placed close together but with enough space between them so the knots will not overlap. Work on evenweave fabric or mark parallel lines for each line of stitches (see p. 53). Work from left to right.

1. Bring the needle to the front of the fabric at A, which is on the edge if the stitch is used as edging.

2. Bring the thread around to the right. Insert the needle at B and bring it out at C, with the thread under the needle at both top and bottom.

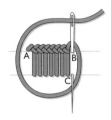

3. Continue as required.

BUTTONHOLE FILLING

This stitch is used to fill large areas. It can be worked with two, three, or four stitches in each group. Work on evenweave fabric or mark parallel lines for each line of stitches required (see p. 53). Work from left to right.

1. Bring the needle to the front of the fabric at A.

2. To make the first stitch, insert the needle in at B and bring it out at C, with the thread below the needle.

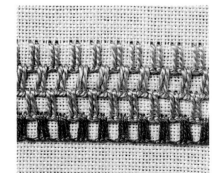

3. Continue to the end of the row, spacing the stitches to form groups of the required number.

4. For the second row, bring the needle out at D, at the right-hand end of the line. Insert the needle at E, overlapping the previous row, and continue to the end of the row.

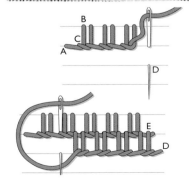

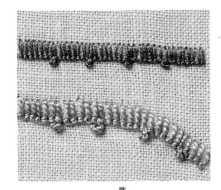

BUTTONHOLE
stitch with picot

In this stitch the picots (knots) can be spaced as required. Work on evenweave fabric or mark two parallel lines for each line of stitches (see p. 53). Work from left to right.

1. Bring the needle to the front of the fabric at A and work the first group of buttonhole stitches (p. 81).

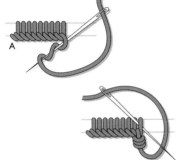

2. Loop the thread around the needle three times, holding it with your thumb, and pull the needle through to make the picot. Take the needle through the last stitch from left to right, sliding it through on top of the fabric.

3. Work the next group of buttonhole stitches and then the next picot, continuing as required.

BUTTONHOLE FLOWER

This stitch is used for flowers and similar designs. For regular shapes, mark two concentric circles. Work in a clockwise direction.

1. Bring the needle to the front of the fabric at A on the inner circle.

2. Insert the needle at B on the outer circle and bring it out at C, keeping the thread under the needle. Keep the stitches on the inner circle small so you have a good number of spokes.

3. Continue around the circle, spacing the spokes regularly.

SINGLE BUTTONHOLE BAR

(Detached buttonhole bar)

The bar is attached to the fabric only at the ends and is used in cutwork. Leave the underlying threads loose to make a curved bar. Two curved bars can be used to make a lens shape. Work from left to right.

1. Bring the needle to the front of the fabric at A, at the left-hand end of the bar. Insert the needle at B, at the right-hand end of the bar, and bring it out at C. Insert it again at D and bring it out just below A.

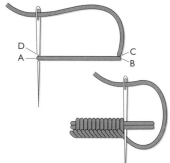

2. Work the buttonhole stitch (p. 81) along the threads, without catching the fabric. The stitches should be close together, and the bar should lie flat.

DOUBLE BUTTONHOLE BAR

This stitch makes a wide, neat-edged bar. On evenweave fabrics, work over a consistent number of threads; on plainweave fabrics, mark two parallel lines for each line of stitches (see p. 53).

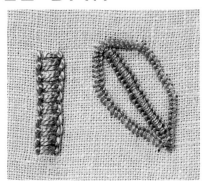

1. Bring the needle to the front of the fabric, at the right-hand end and midway between the two lines. Work a row of running stitch (p. 47).

2. Bring the needle out at the left end of the lower line and work a row of buttonhole stitch (p. 81). The stitches should be close together but with enough space to fit the stitches of the return row.

3. Turn the fabric and work a second row of buttonhole stitches in the spaces.

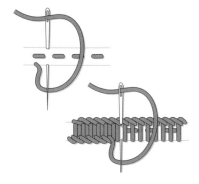

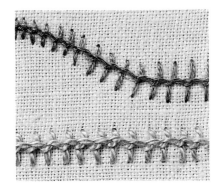

LOOP *stitch*

This stitch is used for straight or curved lines or as filling if the verticals interlock. On evenweave fabrics, work over a consistent number of threads; on plainweave fabrics, mark three parallel lines for each line of stitches (see p. 53). Work from right to left.

1. Bring the needle to the front of the fabric midway between the lines at A.

2. Insert the needle in at B on the upper line and bring it out at C on the lower line.

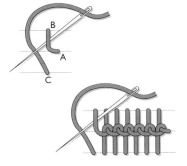

3. Take the needle under the stitch from right to left, sliding it through on top of the fabric and keeping the thread under the needle.

4. Continue as required.

OVERCAST *stitch*

(Straight overcast stitch)

This stitch is used to stitch over an edge for eyelets and in cutwork and buttonholes, as shown.

1. Mark a line or circle and stitch small running stitches (p. 47) around it, finishing with the thread below the running stitches and at the bottom of the shape at A.

2. Cut along the line with small scissors or use an X-acto knife to make a hole along the line between the stitches.

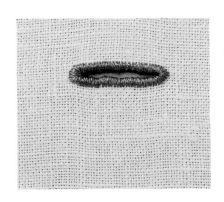

3. Take the needle through the opening or hole and bring it out just to the right of A.

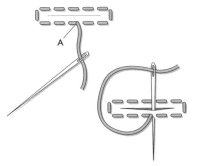

4. Continue as required, keeping the tension even and placing the stitches as close together as possible.

feather stitches

Feather stitches have a delicate, open appearance and are often worked on fine fabric and with only one or two strands of thread. Stitches can be spaced out to look light and feathery or worked closely together for a more solid look.

These stitches are worked on plainweave fabrics, using a crewel needle. For a neat result, keep the angle of the needle and the length and spacing between stitches consistent.

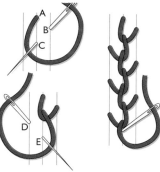

FEATHER *stitch*

Mark three parallel lines on the fabric (see p. 53) and work from top to bottom.

1. Bring the needle to the front of the fabric on the middle line at A. Loop the thread to the right, insert the needle at B, below A but on the right-hand line, and bring it out at C, keeping the thread under the needle.

2. Pull down on the thread and hold it with your thumb. Loop the thread to the left and insert the needle at D. Bring it out at E with the thread under the needle. Continue as required, finishing with a small stitch over the last loop.

LONG-ARMED FEATHER *stitch*

(Cretan stitch)

This stitch is used for edgings and straight or curved lines. Work on evenweave fabric or mark three parallel lines for each line of stitching (see p. 53). Work from top to bottom.

1. Bring the needle to the front on the middle line at A.

2. Loop the thread to the right, insert the needle at B, above A but on the right-hand line and bring it out at C, keeping the thread under the needle. Pull down on the thread and hold it with your thumb. Loop the thread to the left and insert the needle at D. Bring it out at E, with the thread under the needle.

3. Finish with a small stitch over the last loop.

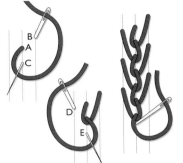

CLOSED FEATHER *stitch*

This stitch is used for straight or curved bands and borders. Work on evenweave fabric or mark two parallel lines for each line of stitches (see p. 53). Work from top to bottom.

1. Bring the needle to the front on the left-hand line at A.

2. Loop the thread to the right. Insert the needle at B and bring it out at C, keeping the thread under the needle. Pull the thread through downward so that the loop rests on the emerging thread.

3. Loop the thread to the left. Insert the needle at A and bring it out at D, with the thread under the needle. Pull through downward as before.

4. Work in the same way, putting the needle in at C and bringing it out at E. Continue working stitches from side to side as required.

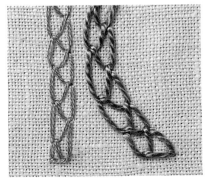

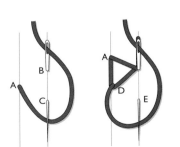

DOUBLE FEATHER
stitch

This stitch is used for zigzag borders. Mark five parallel lines for each line of stitching (see p. 53). Work from top to bottom.

1. Bring the needle to the front at A. Loop the thread to the right. Insert the needle at B, level with A, and bring it out at C, with the thread under the needle.

2. Looping the thread and keeping it under the needle, make another stitch to the left, inserting the needle at D, level with C, and bringing it out at E. Then make another stitch to the left, from F to G.

3. Now make two stitches to the right and two to the left. Continue as required, keeping the stitches level.

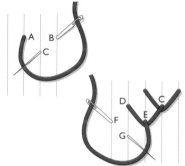

SINGLE FEATHER *stitch*

This stitch is used for borders and in smocking. On evenweave fabrics, work over a consistent number of threads; on plainweave fabrics, mark two parallel lines for each line of stitches (see p. 53). Work from top to bottom.

1. Bring the needle to the front of the fabric on the left-hand line at A.

2. Loop the thread around to the right. Insert the needle at B, on the right-hand line and below A, and bring it out at C, keeping the thread below the needle. Pull the thread through downward.

3. Insert the needle in at D and bring it out at E.

4. Continue as required, making sure the stitches are spaced consistently.

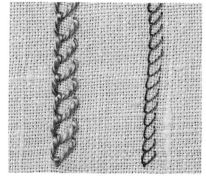

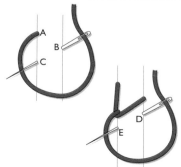

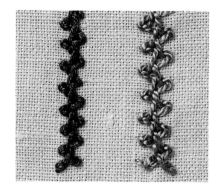

SPANISH KNOTTED FEATHER *stitch*

This stitch is used for borders and gives a braided appearance. The stitches can be spaced out or worked close together. Work on evenweave fabric or mark three parallel lines (see p. 53). Work from top to bottom.

1. Bring the needle to the front of the fabric at A. Loop the thread to the left and insert the needle at B. Bring the needle out at C, within the loop.

2. Loop the thread to the right and insert the needle at D on the middle line and level with A. Bring the needle out at E, within the circle.

3. Continue as required, arranging the loops as you work so that they form a consistent pattern.

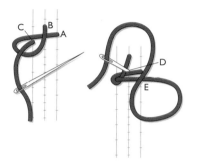

CLOSED FLY *stitch*

This stitch is used for straight or curved bands, or for tapering leaf and feather shapes. For bands, work over a consistent number of threads on evenweave fabrics; on plainweave fabrics, mark three parallel lines for each line of stitches (see p. 53). Work from top to bottom.

1. Bring the needle to the front of the fabric on the middle line at A.

2. Insert the needle at B, below A, and bring it out at C on the left-hand line.

3. Insert the needle at D on the right-hand line and bring it out at B, keeping the thread under the needle.

4. Now insert the needle at E, below B, and bring it out at F, continuing and spacing the stitches as required.

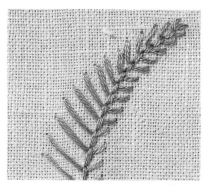

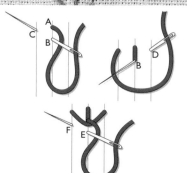

CRETAN *stitch*

This stitch is used for borders and bands. When the verticals are widely spaced, the stitch is sometimes referred to as open Cretan stitch (see top photograph and top two diagrams). When the verticals are closely spaced, it may be called closed Cretan stitch (see lower photograph and lower three diagrams): In this case, it creates a braided center line and can also be used for leaf and feather shapes, see lower photograph. The stitches can be vertical or angled as required. For bands, work over a consistent number of threads on evenweave fabrics; on plainweave fabrics, mark four parallel lines for each line of stitching (see p. 53). Work from left to right or from top to bottom.

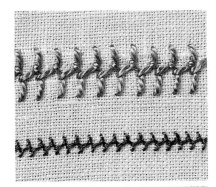

1. Bring the needle to the front of the fabric at A.

2. Loop the thread around to the right. Insert the needle at B and bring it out at C, keeping the thread under the needle.

3. Now, looping the thread around once more, insert the needle at D and bring it out at E, again keeping the thread under the needle.

4. Continue as required, alternating the stitches.

HELPFUL HINT

When you are working horizontally, loop the thread around alternately above and below; when you are working vertically, loop it around alternately to left and right (see diagrams at right).

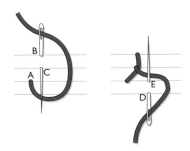

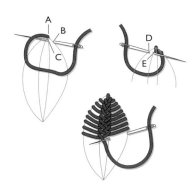

isolated stitches

Isolated stitches are complete in themselves. They can be used singly or grouped to make filling patterns and are especially useful when an irregular or shaded-effect filling is required. Isolated stitches include the various knot stitches, which are used to add a textured dimension to embroidery.

These stitches are most often worked on plainweave fabrics using a crewel needle.

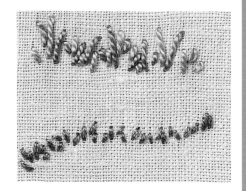

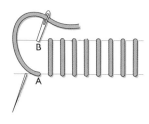

STRAIGHT
stitch

(Single satin stitch)

This stitch is used for short, straight lines or can be used to create patterns. Work from left to right or right to left.

1. Bring the needle to the front of the fabric at A and insert the needle at B.

2. Continue, working consistently and inserting the needle always at the top of the stitch or always at the bottom.

EYELET *stitch*

Eyelets are used singly or scattered across a background, especially in cutwork. The stitches are placed closely together, with a circular or square outline. The same method can be used to work a star with any number of points. Before stitching, the center hole can be enlarged if necessary with a stiletto, which pushes the threads apart without cutting them. On evenweave fabrics, work over a consistent number of threads; on plainweave fabrics, outline the shape required.

1. Bring the needle to the front of the fabric at A.

2. Insert the needle at the center, at B, and bring it out at C. Again, insert the needle at B and bring it out at D.

3. Continue to complete the eyelet.

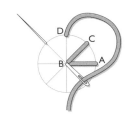

STAR *stitch*

This stitch makes an eight-pointed star and is used singly or scattered across a background. It can be used for large stars because the threads are tied down. Points can be of irregular lengths. For a regular star, work over a consistent number of threads on evenweave fabrics; on plainweave fabrics, outline the star shape required.

1. Bring the needle to the front of the fabric at A. Insert the needle at B and bring it out at C, then in at D and out at E.

2. Now insert the needle at F and bring it out at G, and then insert it at H.

3. Bring the needle out at the center, between spokes G and A, and insert it between spokes B and H, making a small stitch at the center to tie down the threads.

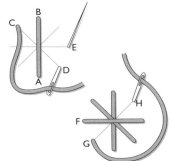

DETACHED CHAIN
stitch
(Lazy daisy stitch, single chain stitch)

This stitch is used alone or in groups, especially to make daisylike flowers and similar shapes, as shown at left.

1. Bring the needle to the front of the fabric at A.

2. Insert the needle at A, looping the thread around to the right, and bring the needle out at B, keeping the thread under the needle.

3. Insert the needle at C to make a small stitch over the thread. This stitch can be lengthened to create a stem.

SEED *stitch*
(Seeding stitch, speckling stitch, isolated back stitch)

This stitch is used for filling, and the stitches are usually scattered irregularly over the area. They are always worked in pairs, and stitches should be quite short.

1. Bring the needle to the front of the fabric at A.

2. Insert the needle at B and bring it up at C, beside A. Insert it at D, close beside B, to complete the stitch.

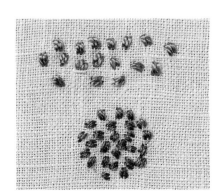

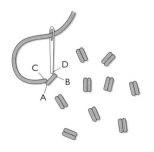

FERN *stitch*

This stitch can be used singly or in vertical or curved rows to create a fernlike effect. The three stitches are usually the same length, but they can be varied if necessary.

1. Bring the needle to the front of the fabric at A and insert it at B.

2. Bring the needle out at C and insert it at B. Then bring it out at D, and again insert it at B to complete the stitch.

3. If required, bring the needle out just below B and continue.

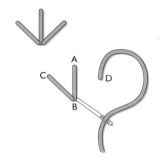

FLY *stitch*

(Open loop stitch)

This stitch is used singly or in rows for a honeycomb effect. As shown at right, it can be worked with a long "tail" to make a Y-shape or a short "tail" for a V-shape.

1. Bring the needle to the front of the fabric at A.

2. Insert the needle at B and leave the thread loose. Bring the needle out at C and insert it at D to anchor the thread.

3. If you are stitching a row, bring the needle out at B and continue, working over an even number of threads or evenly marked lines.

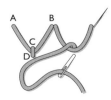

ARROWHEAD *stitch*

This stitch is used singly or in rows as a filling. If working in rows, work over a consistent number of threads on evenweave fabrics; on plainweave fabrics, mark three parallel lines for each line of stitching (see p. 53).

1. Bring the needle to the front of the fabric at A.

2. Insert the needle at B and bring it out at C, level with A, so that C–B is the same distance as A–B.

3. Insert the needle at B.

4. If working a row, bring the needle out at D, level with B, and continue as required.

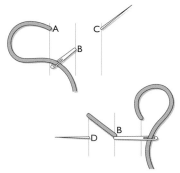

SHEAF *stitch*

(Sheaf filling stitch, faggot filling stitch)

This stitch is used singly or as filling, spaced randomly or in geometric patterns. Rows are worked from right to left.

1. Bring the needle to the front of the fabric at A.

2. Working from right to left, stitch three straight stitches close together, in each case working from bottom to top.

3. Bring the needle out at B, to the left of the last stitch and halfway up it. Take the needle back over the three stitches, then under them from right to left, sliding the needle through on top of the fabric.

4. Take the needle back over the stitches again, then insert it into the fabric under the "sheaf."

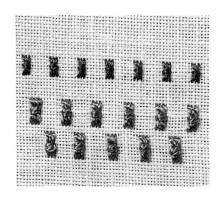

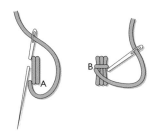

TÊTE DE BOEUF
stitch

This stitch (its name—bull's-head stitch—comes from its shape) consists of a detached chain stitch and two straight stitches. It is used singly or randomly as a filling. For the best results, use a nonstranded thread.

1. Bring the needle to the front of the fabric at A. Insert the needle at A, looping the thread around to the right, and bring the needle out at B, keeping the thread under the needle. Insert the needle at C to make a small stitch over the thread.

2. Bring the needle out at D and insert it at E, then out at F and in at G to complete the stitch.

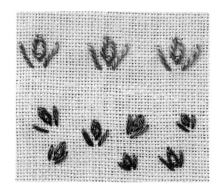

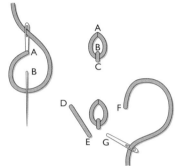

WHEATEAR *stitch*

This stitch consists of a detached chain stitch worked over a horizontal loop of thread. It is used singly as filling or in short vertical rows.

1. Bring the needle to the front of the fabric at A.

2. Loop the thread to the right. Insert the needle at B, level with A, and bring it out at C, with the thread under the needle.

3. Insert the needle beside C, looping the thread around to the right, and bring the needle out at D, keeping the thread under the needle.

4. Insert the needle at E to make a small stitch over the thread.

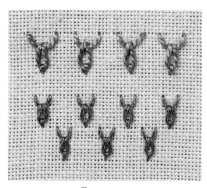

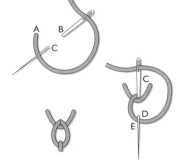

EYELET WHEEL

(Eyelet stitch)

Any number of spokes can be stitched, but if there are more than about ten, the threads at the center of the stitch will not sit neatly. The center hole can be enlarged before stitching with a stiletto if necessary. Work over a consistent number of threads or mark the rim and spokes as required.

1. Bring the needle to the front of the fabric at A, on the rim at the end of a spoke. Insert it at B, at the end of the next spoke, and bring it out at A.

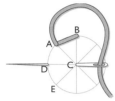

2. Insert the needle at the center, at C, and bring it out at D, then in at A and out at D. Now insert it at C and out at E and continue around the shape until all the spokes and rim are completed.

FOUR-LEGGED KNOT *stitch*

This stitch is used for filling and can be worked in rows or scattered randomly.

1. Bring the needle to the front of the fabric at A.

2 Insert the needle at B and bring it out at C. Lay the thread out to the left in a straight line to form a cross and hold it with your thumb.

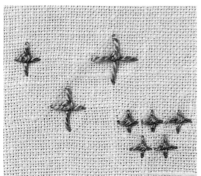

3. With the thread looped around to the bottom, take the needle under the cross from top right to lower left, sliding it under both threads at the center on top of the fabric. Pull it through, keeping the thread under the needle. Tighten the knot.

4. Insert the needle at D to complete the cross.

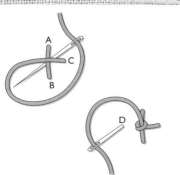

FRENCH KNOT

This stitch is used singly as a raised dot or as filling, either placed closely together or scattered. Traditionally, only one wrap was made, but now two are commonly used. For a neat larger knot, use thicker thread instead of more wraps.

1. Bring the needle to the front of the fabric at A.

2. Hold the thread firmly with the thumb and index finger of your right hand and, with the needle pointing away from the fabric, wrap the thread once or twice around it.

3. Still holding the thread, insert the tip of the needle close to A and slide the wraps down so they lie against the fabric. Pull the thread to tighten the knot around the needle.

4. Hold the wraps with your thumb and insert the needle.

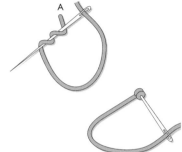

TAILED FRENCH KNOT

This stitch is used singly or in scattered groups. It consists of a French knot with a stem or tail.

1. Bring the needle to the front of the fabric at A.

2. Hold the thread firmly with the thumb and index finger of your left hand and, with the needle pointing away from the fabric, wrap the thread twice around it.

3. Still holding the thread, insert the tip of the needle at B, a short distance from A, and slide the wraps down to the tip of the needle so they lie against the fabric. Pull the thread to tighten the knot around the needle.

4. Hold the wraps with your thumb and push the needle through.

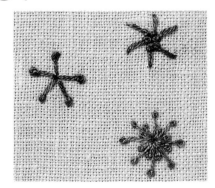

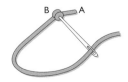

COLONIAL KNOT

(Candlewicking knot)

This stitch makes a knot that is larger than a French knot. It is used singly or worked closely together in lines to form designs (see photograph at left).

1. Bring the needle to the front of the fabric at A.

2. Take the thread over the needle from left to right, bring it up to the left, and hook it under the tip of the needle.

3. Hold the thread taut and insert the tip of the needle close to A.

4. Slide the wraps down, hold them with your thumb, and push the needle through.

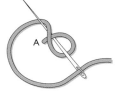

CHINESE KNOT

(Peking knot, forbidden knot, blind knot)

This stitch is used singly or as filling. It is flatter than a French knot. The knot can be pulled closed or left as a small loop.

1. Bring the needle to the front of the fabric at A.

2. Loop the thread to the left. Pick up the loop and fold it over so that the working thread crosses behind the emerging thread.

3. Insert the tip of the needle close to A but within the loop, then tighten the loop around the needle. If required, leave a small loop and hold it with your thumb.

4. Keeping the thread taut, push the needle through.

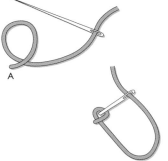

BULLION KNOT

(Worm stitch, caterpillar stitch, coil stitch, roll stitch, post stitch, knot stitch)

This stitch is used singly, as filling, and end-to-end for raised lines. It is commonly used to make bullion roses and rosebuds. Using a straw needle will make the work easier.

1. Bring the needle to the front of the fabric at A.

2. Insert the needle at B (the distance A–B will be the length of the stitch) and bring the needle halfway out at A, taking care not to split the thread.

3. Wrap the thread around the tip of the needle five or six times and pack the wraps down evenly onto the fabric. Hold them in place around the needle and pull the needle through the fabric and the wraps.

4. Pull the thread toward B and use the needle to again pack the wraps into place, making sure they are even and not twisted.

5. Insert the needle at B.

Bullion roses

Roses (see lower photograph) are constructed from a number of separate bullion stitches, beginning with two parallel stitches at the center. Then add one stitch over the top and one more on each side to form a triangle. Continue working rounds, with each stitch overlapping the join between two previous ones. Generally several tones of a color are used, with the darkest at the center.

Rosebuds can be constructed with one stitch at the center and one at either side, sometimes fanning out slightly.

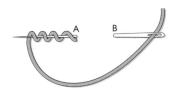

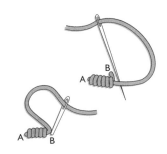

couching stitches

In couching, one or more threads are laid along the surface of the fabric and attached with a series of small stitches, usually in a finer thread. The technique was originally developed so that expensive metallic and silk threads could be used most economically.

The couching, or anchoring, thread can match the laid thread or contrast for a decorative effect. To create an interesting band or border, threads can also be couched using other embroidery stitches, including the various blanket stitches, cross-stitch, chain stitches and herringbone stitch.

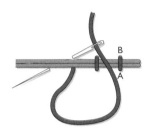

COUCHING

Work from right to left.

1. Bring the laid thread to the front of the fabric and lay it along the line.

2. Bring the anchoring thread to the front at A, below and near the end of the laid thread.

3. Insert the needle at B, just above the laid thread, and bring it out below the thread.

4. Continue, keeping the anchoring stitches spaced evenly. When the line is completed, take the laid thread to the back of the fabric (see Helpful Hint on p. 106).

Changing direction

When laid threads are to change direction, they should be anchored at the turning point.

1. To turn a right-angled corner, make a diagonal stitch across at the turning point (see diagram 1). If the last anchoring stitch fell near the corner and two threads are being couched, it is possible to make the diagonal stitch over the outer laid thread only (see diagram 2).

2. Very sharp corners are best achieved by cutting the laid thread at the corner and taking it to the back of the fabric (see diagram 3). Then bring up a new thread and lay it in the new direction. If two threads are being couched, finish the inner one slightly short of the corner and bring up the new inner thread also short of the outer one.

3. If two threads are being couched around a less sharp corner, they can be anchored by taking only the outer one to the corner and curving the inner one around more gently (see diagram 4). Make an anchoring stitch over the outer thread at the corner. If desired, a separate stitch can be made over the inner thread.

Couched circles

This method can be used for a single laid thread or for two threads, laid side by side, with the anchoring stitches worked over both threads at the same time.

1. On the fabric, mark regularly spaced spokes from the center of the circle. Bring the thread to be laid to the front of the fabric at the center of the circle.

2. Bring the anchoring thread to the front on the outside edge of the laid thread. Curl the laid thread around in a tight circle and make small anchoring stitches over it,

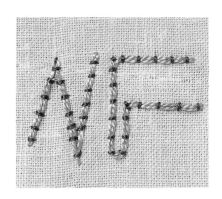

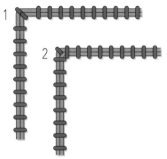

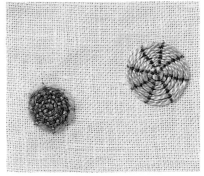

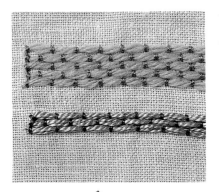

working always from the outside toward the center and placing a stitch on each alternate spoke.

3. Continue curling the laid thread around and, on the second round, make a small stitch over it at each spoke, as shown at right in the photograph.

4. For a bricked effect, as shown in the upper part of the diagram, on the next round place the stitches midway between the spokes, and on the fourth round place them on the spokes, continuing as required. For a radiating effect, continue as for the second round, placing all the stitches on the spokes, as shown in the lower part of the diagram.

5. Take the laid threads to the back of the fabric and tuck them under the previous round.

BRICKING

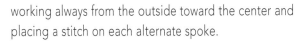

This stitch is used for filling. For a consistent pattern on evenweave fabrics, count threads; on plainweave fabrics, mark parallel lines of dots as a guide for each line of stitching (see p. 53). Start from the top right, working backward and forward.

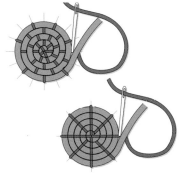

1. Bring the thread to be laid to the front of the fabric and lay it along the line (or thread, if using evenweave fabric).

2. Bring the anchoring thread to the front, below and near the end of the laid thread, and work anchoring stitches along the line.

3. Turn the laid thread, placing it alongside the first row, and work a horizontal anchoring stitch at the turn.

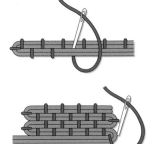

4. Turn the fabric around and continue, placing each stitch midway between those of the previous row.

BUNCHED COUCHING

This stitch is used for couching a number of separate strands to create a wide, decorative line (see p. 53). Work from right to left.

1. Bring the threads to be laid to the front of the fabric and lay them along the line. Hold them in place.

2. Bring the couching thread to the front at A, below and near the ends of the laid threads.

3. Insert the needle at B, just above the laid threads, and bring it out to the left and below the threads. Pull the laid threads, so that they bunch up between the anchoring stitches.

4. Continue, spacing the stitches evenly.

PENDANT COUCHING

(Looped couching)

This stitch can be worked with a closed or open loop. Work from right to left. When filling an area, start at the bottom right and work backward and forward.

1. Bring the thread to be couched to the front of the fabric and hold it in place.

2. Bring the anchoring thread to the front at A, below and near the end of the laid thread. Insert the needle at B, just above the laid thread.

3. Arrange the laid thread in a loop (open or closed, as shown at right) and make a small anchoring stitch over it. The stitches should be close together.

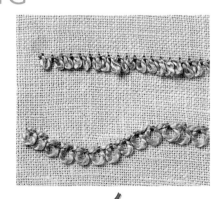

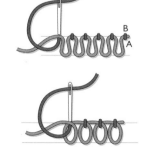

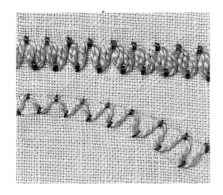

ZIGZAG COUCHING

This stitch is used for straight or curved decorative lines. On evenweave fabrics, work over a consistent number of threads; on plainweave fabrics, mark two parallel lines to keep the stitches regular (see p. 53). Work from right to left.

1. Bring the thread to be laid to the front of the fabric on the upper line and hold it in place.

2. Bring the anchoring thread to the front at A. Insert the needle at B to make a vertical stitch over the laid thread.

3. Angle the laid thread down to the lower line and make a vertical stitch over it from C to D.

4. Continue, spacing the stitches evenly.

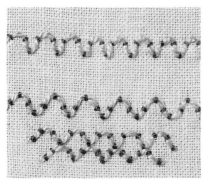

FISH-SCALE COUCHING

This stitch is used for wavy lines or filling with a fish-scale effect. On plainweave fabrics, mark parallel lines of dots to keep the stitches regular. More anchoring stitches may be used for larger scales. Start at the top-left corner and work backward and forward.

1. Bring the laid thread to the front of the fabric at the left end of the second line and hold it in place. Bring the anchoring thread to the front at A and insert the needle in at B to make a stitch.

2. Curve the laid thread up to the top line and back down, taking anchoring stitches from C to D and from E to F. Make another anchoring stitch at the base of the curve and continue to the right.

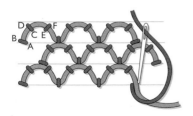

BOKHARA COUCHING

This stitch is used as filling. The same thread is used for the laid threads and the anchoring stitches to create the textured look. Mark the outline of the area to be covered on the fabric, as well as any pattern to be made by the anchoring stitches (see photographs and diagrams at right). Work from the bottom upward.

1. Bring the thread to be couched to the front of the fabric at A, at the bottom-left corner of the area, and hold it in place with your thumb.

2. Insert the needle at B, at the right-hand end of the marked area. The thread should lie loosely on the fabric. Bring the needle out at C for the first anchoring stitch.

3. Insert the needle at D to make a small, firm diagonal stitch and bring it out at E for the next anchoring stitch. Continue to the end of the row.

4. Bring the needle out at F, just above A, so that no fabric is visible, and continue as required.

HELPFUL HINT

The ends of laid threads are secured by plunging. First, take the end of the thread to the back of the fabric, if necessary making a hole with a stiletto, carefully pushing the fabric threads apart without breaking them. A thick cord may be unraveled and each strand taken back separately. Secure the ends with the anchoring thread and clip close to the fabric.

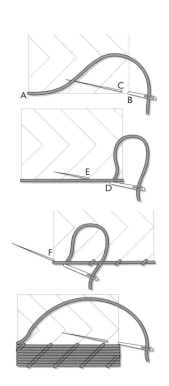

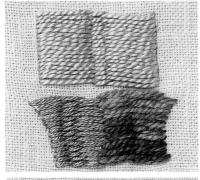

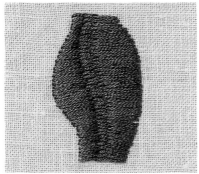

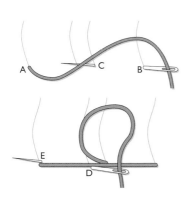

ROMANIAN COUCHING

(Romanian couching, Oriental laid stitch, antique couching, figure stitch)

This stitch is used as filling for large areas and gives a smooth appearance, with the long anchoring stitches forming a distinct pattern. The same thread is used for the laid threads and the anchoring stitches. Mark the outline of the area on the fabric, as well as parallel lines for the anchoring stitches. Work from the bottom upward.

1. Bring the thread to the front of the fabric at A, at the bottom-left corner of the area, and hold it in place.

2. Insert the needle at B, at the right-hand end of the area. The thread should lie loosely on the fabric. Bring the needle out at C for the first anchoring stitch.

3. Insert the needle at D to make a firm diagonal stitch and bring it out at E, just above A, so that no fabric is visible. Continue as required.

HELPFUL HINT

When couching, the fabric must be taut so that the laid thread remains flat. Always use an embroidery hoop or frame.

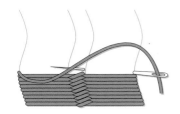

TRAILING

This stitch makes a raised, cordlike line and can be worked over a firm, round thread or bundle of threads. Work from left to right.

1. Bring the thread to be couched to the front of the fabric and hold it in place.

2. Bring the anchoring thread to the front at A and insert the needle at B. Pick up as little fabric as possible before bringing the needle out right beside A.

3. Continue stitching, covering the laid thread to the end of the line. The anchoring stitches should completely cover the laid thread. When the line is completed, take the thread to the back of the fabric.

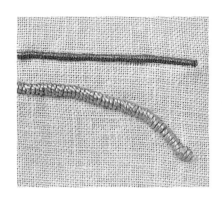

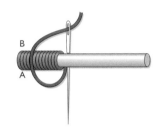

THORN *stitch*

This stitch is a decorative form of false couching because it is worked with a single thread. It is used for foliage effects. For a neat pattern on evenweave fabrics, work over a consistent number of threads; on plainweave fabrics, mark three parallel lines for each line of stitches (see p. 53). Work from bottom to top.

1. Bring the thread to the front of the fabric and work a long, straight, vertical stitch along the line to be embroidered.

2. Bring the needle out at A, level with the lower end of the straight stitch.

3. Insert the needle at B and bring it out at C, level with A. Now insert it at D, level with B, and bring it out at E.

4. Continue as required.

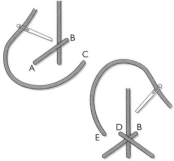

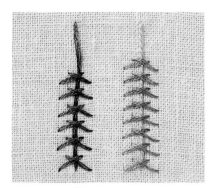

TRELLIS *stitch*

(Trellis filling, square laid filling, squared laidwork)

The squares created by this stitch can be decorated with isolated stitches. Mark a regular grid on plainweave fabrics (see p. 53).

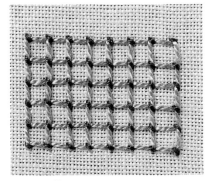

1. Bring the thread to be couched to the front of the fabric at the top left (or right) and work long, straight horizontal stitches. Then start at the lower-left or lower-right corner and make similar vertical stitches across the area. Take the thread to the back.

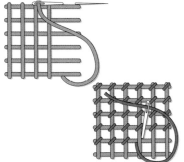

2. Working from the top left (or right), bring the anchoring thread to the front of the fabric and work a small diagonal stitch across each intersection, as shown at left.

JACOBEAN COUCHING

(Trellis couching)

This stitch is used for filling curved shapes such as leaves. Mark a regular grid in the desired shape on plainweave fabrics (see p. 53).

1. Bring the thread to be couched to the front of the fabric and cover the area with horizontal and vertical stitches (see above, trellis stitch, step 1).

2. Starting from the top left (or right), bring the anchoring thread to the front of the fabric and work a small diagonal stitch across each intersection of the first row. Work back along the same row, making a diagonal stitch across each intersection to form crosses.

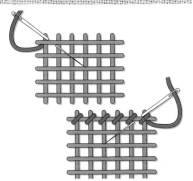

3. Repeat for each row, keeping all the top diagonals in the same direction.

DIAGONAL LAID FILLING

(Laidwork trellis, trellis filling)

The anchoring stitches can be vertical or horizontal. Mark a regular diagonal grid on plainweave fabrics (see p. 53).

1. Bring the thread to the front of the fabric at A and insert it at B. Bring it out at C and insert it at D to make a double line. Continue making parallel double lines as required. Then bring the thread up at E and work corresponding double lines back the other way.

2. Bring the anchoring thread up at F and insert it at G, and continue across the first row of intersections. Then work back the other way, anchoring all intersections.

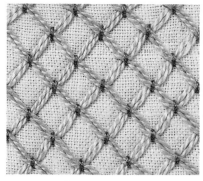

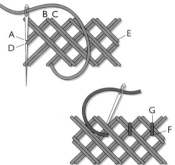

TRELLIS AND CROSS FILLING

This stitch is used as filling for regular and irregular areas. Use a hoop to hold the fabric taut and mark a regular diagonal grid on plainweave fabrics (see p. 53).

1. Bring the thread to be couched to the front of the fabric near the top left and work a diagonal stitch to the top. Make a parallel stitch to the right. Continue making parallel double lines as required. Then work corresponding double lines back the other way.

2. Bring the anchoring thread to the front at A and insert it at B, in the center of the intersection. Then work from C to B, D to B, and E to B to complete the cross. Continue, making a cross over each intersection and working the stitches in the same order for a consistent appearance.

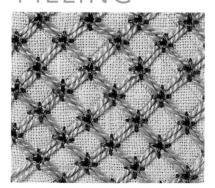

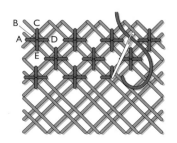

BATTLEMENT COUCHING

(Battlement filling)

This stitch is usually worked in three blending colors. Mark a regular grid on plainweave fabrics (see p. 53).

1. Using the first color of thread, make a series of evenly spaced horizontal lines. Then make vertical lines over them.

2. Bring the second thread to the front and repeat, placing the stitches just above and to the right of the first grid. Repeat with the third thread, as shown at left.

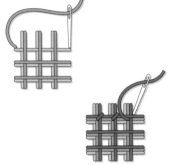

3. Using the third-color thread, bring the needle up at the top-left intersection and make anchoring stitches over the third grid only.

SQUARE AND DIAGONAL FILLING

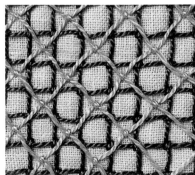

This stitch is usually worked in two blending colors. Mark a regular grid on plainweave fabrics (see p. 53).

1. Bring the first-color thread to the front of the fabric at the top left and work the trellis stitch (p. 109) over the area, with the anchoring stitches in the same color as the grid.

2. Bring the second-color thread to the front at A and insert it at B. Then bring it out at C and insert it at D. Continue making diagonal stitches back and forth across the area. Then repeat in the opposite direction (see upper part of diagram).

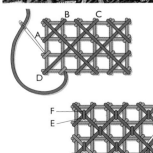

3. Using the same color thread, bring the needle up at E and insert it at F. Continue making vertical anchoring stitches over the intersections of the diagonal grid, working each stitch in the same direction.

TRIANGLE FILLING

This stitch covers an area with a pattern of triangular shapes. Mark a regular triangular grid on plainweave fabrics (see p. 53).

1. Bring the thread to the front of the fabric at A and insert it at B. Bring it out at C and insert it at D, continue to make parallel diagonal lines across the area (see diagram 1).

2. Repeat step 1 in the opposite direction, placing the needle on the outside of the first stitches (see diagram 2).

3. In the same way, make horizontal stitches across the area, starting at the bottom and working from left to right. The horizontal stitches should pass over the intersections of the diagonal grid (see diagram 3).

4. Bring the anchoring thread to the front at E and insert it at F. Make a small vertical stitch across each intersection, working each stitch from bottom to top for a regular appearance (see diagram 4).

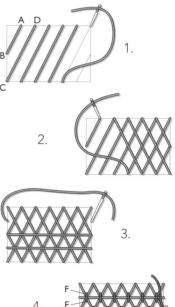

satin stitches

Satin stitches provide a smooth filling for smaller areas and look especially attractive when worked in a glossy thread, such as stranded embroidery cottons. They are often used for the different elements in floral or landscape scenes.

It is essential to keep an even tension when working these stitches. Using an embroidery hoop and the stab method of stitching with a crewel needle will give the most even results. Also, the stitches should not be too long, or you will find it difficult to keep them neat and even.

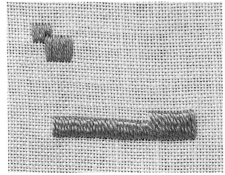

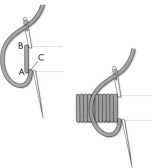

SATIN *stitch*

(Damask stitch)

This stitch can be worked vertically or horizontally. Working around the shape, just inside the edge, in a split stitch (p. 50) forms a firm base and keeps the outline neat, especially for irregular shapes. Work from left to right.

1. Bring the needle to the front of the fabric at A. Insert the needle at B and bring it out at C, right beside A, so that no fabric shows between the stitches.

2. Continue as required, keeping the stitches close together and parallel, to ensure the outline remains neat.

SLANTED SATIN
stitch

Working a base of split stitch (p. 50) around the desired shape helps keep the outline neat. The stitch can be worked from left or right and the direction can be varied so that the threads catch the light in different ways.

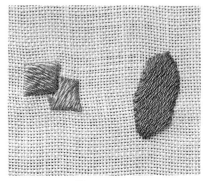

1. Bring the needle to the front of the fabric at A, in the center of the shape. Insert the needle at B, so the stitch slants at 45 degrees. Bring it out beside A, so that no fabric shows between the stitches.

2. Continue stitching to the edge of the shape, keeping the stitches close together and parallel, and make sure the outline remains neat. Return to the center of the shape and work to the left.

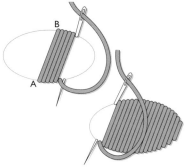

ENCROACHING SATIN *stitch*

This stitch is used as filling for areas that are too large for the normal satin stitch. It can be worked in several color values. Mark the edge of each row on the fabric for a neat result. Work from left to right.

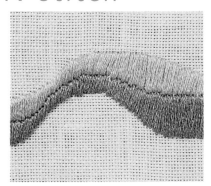

1. Bring the needle to the front of the fabric at A.

2. Insert the needle at B and bring it out beside A, so that no fabric shows between the stitches.

3. Continue stitching to the end of the row, keeping the stitches close together and parallel, and make sure that the outline remains neat.

4. Bring the thread to the front again at C and insert the needle at D, slightly overlapping and between the two stitches of the previous row. Continue stitching as for the first row.

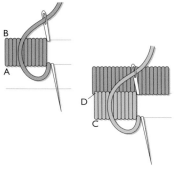

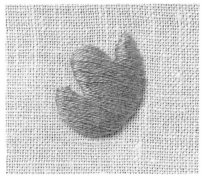

PADDED SATIN
stitch

This stitch is used to fill small areas and gives a raised effect. This is achieved by stitching the satin stitch over a bottom layer of stitches (see top photograph) or nonwoven fabric such as interfacing or felt (see lower photograph).

Stitch padding
Use the same color thread for all layers of stitching.

1. Stitch around the shape using the split stitch (see diagram 1).

2. Fill the shape with small chain, stem (p. 48), or running (p. 47) stitches, working in a different direction to the final satin stitch (see diagram 2). Alternatively, cover the shape with the satin stitch (p. 113), again in a different direction to the final layer, but stitching over the split-stitch outline.

3. Cover the shape with satin stitch (see diagrams 3 and 4). Begin in the center and work toward one end; then work from the center toward the other end.

Fabric padding

1. Cut nonwoven fabric to fit inside the shape and sew it in place with small stitches (or use iron-on interfacing).

2. Work the satin stitch (p. 113) over the fabric, keeping the outline even and neat.

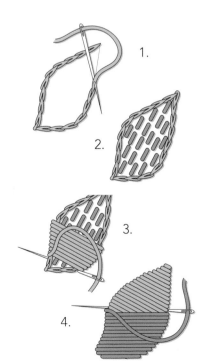

1.

2.

3.

4.

LONG-AND-SHORT *stitch*

(Long-and-short satin stitch, plumage stitch, shading stitch)

This stitch is used as filling and allows a gradual shading of colors. For irregular shapes or on plainweave fabric, mark guidelines on the fabric (see p. 53). Work from left to right and top to bottom. All long stitches are the same length.

1. Bring the needle to the front of the fabric at A.

2. Insert the needle at B and bring it out at C. Continue to the right, making alternate short and long stitches. Keep the stitches parallel and make sure that no fabric shows between stitches.

3. Bring the needle up at D to make a long stitch and insert it at E, splitting the base of the stitch above if necessary. Then bring it out at F and insert it at G in the same way. Make long stitches to the end of the second row.

4. Stitch as many rows of long stitches as required, finishing with a row of long and short stitches.

Shaping

1. Bring the needle to the front of the fabric at A, on the long side of the shape (see lower diagram).

2. Work one row of long and short stitches to the right edge of the shape; then work from the center to the left edge, slanting the stitches as required to fit the shape.

3. Work as many rows of long stitches as required, slanting them in, so there are fewer stitches in each row.

4. If necessary, work a final row of long and short stitches to complete the shape.

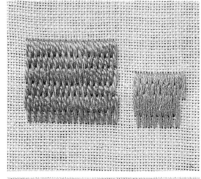

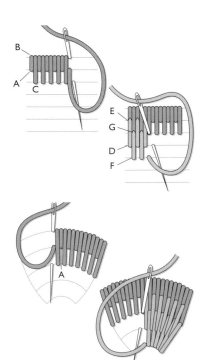

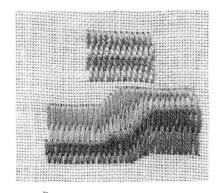

PLATE *stitch*

This stitch produces an interlocking pattern that does not completely cover the fabric. For the best results, mark parallel lines on plainweave fabric (see p. 53). Work from left to right.

1. Bring the needle to the front of the fabric at A. Insert the needle at B and bring it up at C. Then insert it at D, as shown at left in the diagram.

2. Bring the needle out at E and put it in level with B, as shown in the middle of the diagram. Continue stitching to the end of the row, keeping each stitch vertical.

3. For the next row, again bring the needle up at the left end and slightly above the bottom of the stitches of the previous row, as seen at right in the diagram. Continue as required.

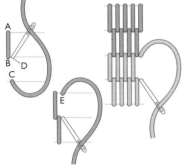

BRICK *stitch*

This stitch has a subtle basketweave pattern. On plainweave fabrics, mark parallel lines (see p. 53). Work from left to right and top to bottom.

1. Bring the needle to the front of the fabric at A.

2. Insert the needle at B and bring it out at C. Continue to the end of the row, making alternate short and long stitches. Keep the stitches parallel and close together so that no fabric shows between the stitches.

3. Bring the needle up at the right end of the next row, at D, and insert it at the bottom of the previous row at E. Continue working long stitches to the end of the row.

4. Work additional rows as required, stitching backward and forward. Work a final row of long and short stitches.

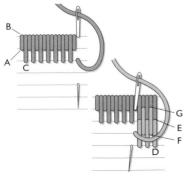

woven stitches

Woven stitches consist of a base embroidery stitch worked through the fabric and then a second layer of thread woven through the base stitches without piercing the fabric. Depending on the effect required, the woven thread can match the base thread or be a different color.

The base stitch is worked with a crewel needle, but the weaving is done with a tapestry needle, which is less likely to catch the fabric as it slides through.

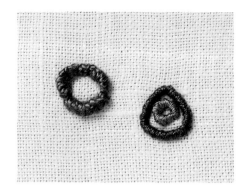

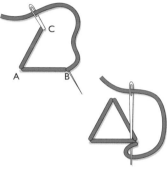

RAISED CUP
stitch

This stitch is worked on a triangular base to create a raised circle or "cup."

1. Bring the needle to the front at A. Insert it at B, out at C, then in at A, out at B, and in at C to make a raised triangle.

2. Bring the thread out just below B and change to a tapestry needle. Take the thread around to the right and slide the needle under the first stitch from top to bottom, with the thread under the needle. Work around the triangle clockwise, placing stitches close beside each other.

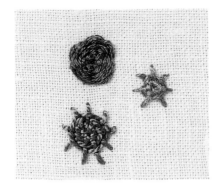

WOVEN WHEEL

This stitch is used for small, raised circles. Mark the center and an odd number of spokes on the fabric.

1. Bring the needle to the front of the fabric at the outside of one spoke and work a straight stitch over each spoke.

2. Using a tapestry needle, bring the needle out at A and take it over the first spoke and under the next, taking care not to catch the fabric.

3. Continue weaving around the spokes, making sure that the threads lie flat. To finish, insert the needle under the last round and take the thread to the back.

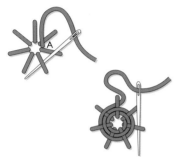

SPIDER WEB

(Whipped circle)

This stitch is used for small, raised circles. Mark the center and an odd number of spokes on the fabric.

1. Bring the needle to the front at the outside of one spoke and work a straight stitch to the center over each spoke.

2. Using a tapestry needle, bring the needle out at A. Slide it under the spoke and then bring it back and slide it under the same spoke and the next one. Take care not to catch the fabric.

3. Bring the needle back and pass it under the second and third spokes, continuing as required around the circle.

4. To finish, insert the needle under the last round and take the thread to the back.

BUTTONHOLE LOOP

(Detached blanket stitch)

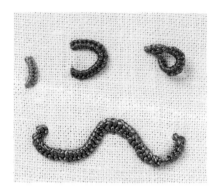

This stitch features the buttonhole stitch to make a loop that sits on the surface of the fabric. It can be used as a button loop. Work from left to right.

1. Bring the needle to the front of the fabric at A and insert it at B, keeping the thread loose. Repeat from C to D, bringing the needle up just below C.

2. Using a tapestry needle, work the buttonhole stitch (p. 81) over the threads, keeping the stitches close together and making sure that they do not catch the fabric.

3. To finish, insert the needle just below D.

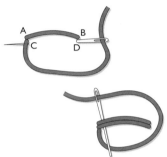

TWISTED BUTTONHOLE LOOP

(Twisted detached blanket stitch)

In this loop, the buttonhole stitch is twisted in the center to give a sinuous effect. Work from left to right.

1. Make two straight stitches and leave them loose (see diagrams above). Bring the needle up just below the left end.

2. Using a tapestry needle, work the buttonhole stitch (p. 81) halfway along the loop. Keep the stitches close together and make sure that they do not catch the fabric.

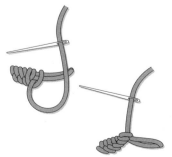

3. Work another buttonhole stitch, but when the loop is not quite closed, pull the thread upward and away from you so that the ridge begins to turn. Repeat to the end of the loop so that the ridge gradually twists around. Insert the needle just above the end of the loop.

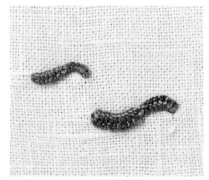

WOVEN PICOT

This stitch is used for small shapes such as leaves. It is a raised stitch, attached only at the base. Use a tapestry needle when working the picot (knot).

1. Use a pin to mark the center line of the picot, as shown in diagram 1.

2. Bring the needle to the front of the fabric at A, take it around the pin, and insert it at B.

3. Bring the needle out at C and take the thread around the pin. Slide the needle under the right-hand side of the first loop from right to left without catching the fabric. Then weave it over itself and under the left-hand side of the first loop, also shown in diagram 1.

4. Now bring the needle back over the left-hand side of the first loop, under the stem of the second loop, and over the right-hand side of the first loop, gently pushing the weaving toward the pin.

5. Continue weaving back and forth until you reach the bottom, taking care not to catch the fabric. To finish, insert the needle behind the last thread, near B, as shown in diagram 2.

HELPFUL HINT

When working woven stitches, don't pull the thread through too tightly. Keep the tension consistent and arrange the weaving as you go to ensure even results.

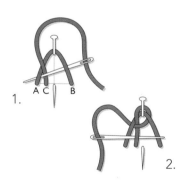

WHIPPING

Whipping is worked over a base stitch using a contrasting thread color and without piercing the fabric. It is used for decorative straight and curved lines. Whipping can be used over many stitches, including the running stitch (p. 47), back stitch (p. 48), stem stitch (p. 48), chain stitch (p. 54), couched threads (pp. 101–12), and blanket stitch (p. 75).

The top photograph shows the whipped running stitch (top three lines) and the whipped back stitch (lower two lines), while the lower photograph shows the whipped stem stitch (top), whipped chain stitch (center), and whipped blanket stitch (lower). The method is the same in all cases. Use a tapestry needle for whipping and work from right to left or top to bottom.

1. Work a line of the desired base stitch.

2. Bring the contrasting thread to the front of the fabric at A, below the first stitch.

3. Take the needle under each stitch from top to bottom, sliding it through on top of the fabric, as shown at right.

4. At the end of the row, take the needle to the back of the fabric above the last stitch.

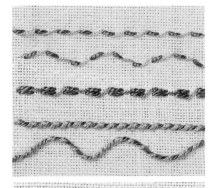

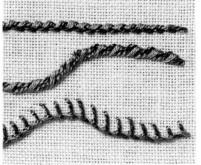

Whipped running stitch

Whipped blanket stitch

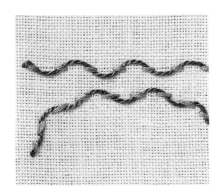

LACED RUNNING
stitch

This stitch is worked using contrasting thread colors and is done without piercing the fabric. Use a tapestry needle for lacing. Work from right to left.

1. Work a line of running stitch (p. 47).

2. Bring the contrasting thread to the front of the fabric at A, below the first running stitch (see upper diagram).

3. Take the needle under each stitch, alternating from bottom to top and from top to bottom, sliding it through on top of the fabric (see lower diagram).

4. At the end of the row, take the needle to the back of the fabric above or below the last stitch.

THREADED BACK *stitch*

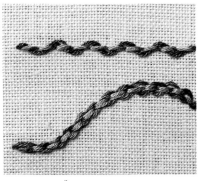

This stitch is worked using contrasting thread colors. Work from right to left.

1. Work a line of back stitch in the first thread color (see p. 48).

2. Using a tapestry needle, bring the contrasting thread to the front of the fabric, below the first back stitch. Take the needle under each stitch, alternating from bottom to top and from top to bottom, sliding it through on top of the fabric (see upper diagram).

3. At the end of the row, take the needle to the back of the fabric above or below the last stitch.

Double-threaded backstitch
Work a second row of threading, starting above the first stitch (see lower diagram).

PEKINESE *stitch*

(Chinese stitch)

This stitch is worked using contrasting thread colors. It is used for braidlike straight and curved lines. Work from left to right, keeping the loops the same size.

1. Work a line of back stitch in the first thread color (see p. 48).

2. Using a tapestry needle and the second color, bring the thread to the front of the fabric at A. Take the needle under the second back stitch, slipping it through on top of the fabric, and then back under the first back stitch to form a loop, as shown in the diagram.

3. Now slip the needle under the third backstitch and back under the second. Continue as required.

THREADED HERRINGBONE *stitch*

This stitch is worked using contrasting thread colors. On evenweave fabric, work over a consistent number of threads; on plainweave fabric, mark two parallel lines (see p. 53). Use a tapestry needle for threading. Work from right to left.

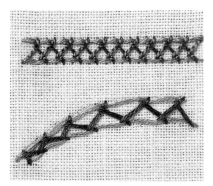

1. Work a row of herringbone stitch (p. 72). Bring the contrasting thread to the front of the fabric at A, as shown in the diagram below.

2. Working above the top intersections, take the needle under the right diagonal and over the left one, sliding it through on top of the fabric. Continue to the end of the row and take the thread to the back.

3. Bring a new thread up at B and repeat below the lower intersections.

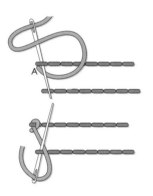

HERRINGBONE LADDER *stitch*

This stitch is used for borders with a twisted appearance. It can be worked in one or two colors. On evenweave fabric, work over a consistent number of threads; on plainweave fabric, mark two parallel lines (see p. 53).

1. Work two rows of back stitch (p. 48) along the marked lines. Keep the stitches the same length, but stagger them so that they are not aligned.

2. Using a tapestry needle, bring the second-color thread to the front of the fabric at the left end of the upper line, at A, as shown in the upper diagram.

3. Loop the thread around to the right and take the needle under the first stitch from top to bottom, with the thread under the needle.

4. Again, keeping the thread to the right, take the needle under the first stitch on the lower line, from bottom to top, with the thread under the needle, as shown in the middle diagram.

5. Continue to the end of the row.

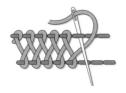

INTERLACED RUNNING *stitch*

This stitch is worked using contrasting thread colors. It is used for broad bands and in close rows for filling. Use a tapestry needle for lacing. Work from right to left.

1. Work two lines of running stitch (p. 47) with the stitches aligned.

2. Bring the contrasting thread to the front of the fabric at A, below the first running stitch on the lower line. Take the needle under each pair of stitches, alternating from bottom to top and from top to bottom, sliding it through on top of the fabric, as shown in the diagram at right.

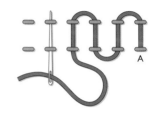

3. At the end of the row, take the needle to the back of the fabric above or below the last stitch.

INTERLACED CHAIN *stitch*

This stitch is worked using contrasting thread colors. Work from top to bottom. Use a tapestry needle.

1. Work a row of chain stitch in the first thread color (see p. 54). Bring the contrasting thread to the front of the fabric at A, at the top of the row, as shown in the diagram below.

2. Working down the right side, take the needle from right to left under the second stitch, bringing it up in the middle of the stitch. Then take it from left to right under the right side of the first stitch and contrasting thread. Slide it under the third chain and back under the second. Continue to base.

3. Bring a new thread up at A and work down the left side, taking the needle from left to right under the second chain and then from right to left under the first chain and contrasting thread.

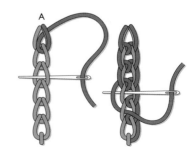

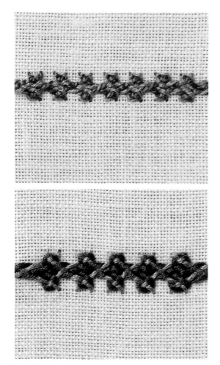

INTERLACED HERRINGBONE BAND

This stitch makes intricate decorative bands or borders. It is worked over a row of double herringbone stitch (p. 74) using contrasting thread colors. On evenweave fabric, work over a consistent number of threads; on plainweave fabric, mark two parallel lines for each line of stitching (see p. 53). Work from left to right, using a tapestry needle.

1. Work a row of double herringbone stitch, leaving the stitches at either end shorter.

2. Bring the contrasting thread to the front of the fabric at A, at the base of the first intersection, as shown in diagram 1.

3. Take the needle over the first diagonal and under the second, and then weave in around the top intersection, as shown in diagram 2, over the first diagonal, then under both the second diagonal and itself to come out at the base of the next intersection on the same level as A. Continue to the end of the row.

4. Weave around the final intersection and work back along the bottom of the herringbone, weaving under and over both the herringbone diagonals and the contrasting thread, as shown in diagram 3.

5. Finish by taking the thread to the back, close to A, as shown in diagram 4.

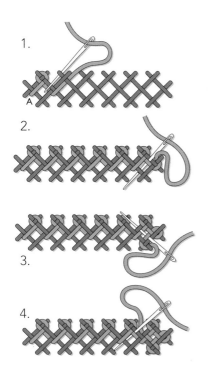

1.

2.

3.

4.

INTERLACED HERRINGBONE *stitch*

(Laced herringbone stitch)

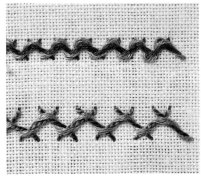

This stitch is worked using contrasting thread colors. It is used for broad bands and in close rows as filling. Work from left to right. Use a tapestry needle.

1. Work a row of herringbone stitch (p. 72).

2. Bring the contrasting thread to the front at A, on the outside of the stitch, then over it to the right. Take the needle under the first diagonal from bottom to top and then under the second from top to bottom, without piercing the fabric. Continue to the end of the row and finish by inserting the needle on the inside of the base of the last diagonal.

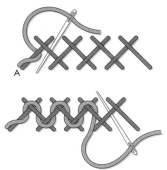

RAISED STEM *stitch*

(Raised stem band)

In this stitch the straight stitches can be covered or show at either side. (Two colors may be used.) For an even band, as shown in the photograph at right, work on evenweave fabric, or mark two parallel lines (see p. 53).

1. Bring a crewel needle to the front at A, insert it at B, and bring it out at C. Continue to work straight stitches.

2. Using a tapestry needle, bring the second-color thread to the front at the bottom at D and take it over and then under the second straight stitch, sliding it through on top of the fabric and bringing the needle out to the left. Continue over each straight stitch.

3. Add additional rows of stem stitch as required.

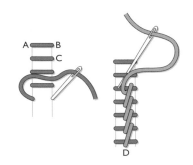

RAISED CHAIN
stitch

(Raised chain band)

This stitch makes a broad decorative band, with rows of chain stitch worked over a series of straight stitches. Each row of chain stitch may be worked over a separate "ladder" if desired. The straight stitches can be covered or show at either side. (Two colors may be used.) For an even band, work on evenweave fabric or mark two parallel lines for each line of stitching on plainweave fabric (see p. 53). Use a tapestry needle.

1. Bring a crewel needle to the front of the fabric at A, insert it at B, and bring it out at C. Continue to work a series of straight stitches, as shown in diagram 1.

2. Using a tapestry needle, bring the second thread to the front at the top, at D, and take it over and then under the first stitch, sliding it through on top of the fabric and bringing it out to the left, as shown in diagram 2.

3. Bring the thread around in a loop and slide the needle under the first stitch again, bringing it out with the thread under the needle, as shown in diagram 3.

4. Repeat this on the next straight stitch and then continue, working each chain stitch in the same way. Make a small vertical stitch over the last straight stitch to secure.

1.

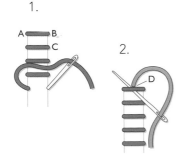

2.

3.

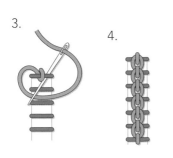

4.

PORTUGUESE BORDER *stitch*

This stitch is used for a band or border with serrated edges. On evenweave fabrics, work over a consistent number of threads; on plainweave fabrics, mark two parallel lines for each line of stitching (see p. 53).

1. Bring a crewel needle to the front of the fabric at A and insert it at B. Then bring it out at C and insert it at D. Continue to work a series of straight stitches, as shown in diagram 1.

2. Using a tapestry needle, bring a second thread to the front at E, below the bottom straight stitch and to the right of center. Take it over the second stitch and slide it under both stitches on top of the fabric. Repeat twice, working toward the left, as shown in diagram 2.

3. Again take the needle over the second stitch, but bring it out below the second stitch, to the left, as shown in diagram 3.

4. Place the needle under the third stitch near the center and slide it under that and the second stitch, slanting this stitch to the right. Slide it under the third stitch only and continue working up the left side of the ladder.

5. At the top of the ladder, complete the two stitches and take the needle to the back of the fabric.

6. Bring a new thread to the front of the fabric at F, as shown in diagram 4, left and work stitches up the right side of the ladder in the same way, slanting them to the left.

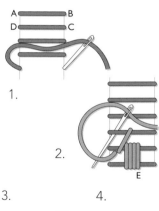

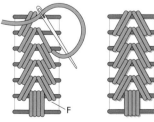

1.

2.

3.

4.

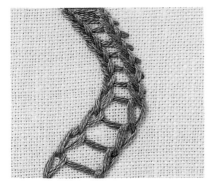

LADDER *stitch*

This stitch is used for a straight or curving band. On evenweave fabrics, work over a consistent number of threads; on plainweave fabrics, mark two parallel lines for each line of stitching, as shown in the diagrams at left (see p. 53). Work from top to bottom. Use a tapestry needle.

1. Bring the thread to the front of the fabric at A, as shown in diagram 1.

2. Insert the needle at B and bring it out at C, just above B. Insert it at D, just below B, and bring it out at E, just below A, as shown in diagram 2.

3. Slide the needle under the left-hand end of the stitch from top to bottom, with the thread under the needle. Take care not to catch the fabric.

4. Take the needle back to the other side and slide it under both stitches from right to left, as shown in diagram 3.

5. Insert the needle at F, a little below D, and bring it out at G, as shown in diagram 4.

6. Take the needle between the two horizontal stitches at left and slide it under the knot from right to left, without catching the fabric, as shown in diagram 5.

7. Take the needle back to the other side and slide it under the knot from right to left, as shown in diagram 6.

8. Continue as required.

1.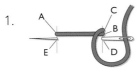

2.

3.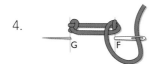

4.

5.

6.

woven filling

Woven filling stitches consist of a grid of short or long stitches worked over the area to be filled, and then a layer of thread is woven into them without piercing the fabric. The effect can be open or closed, depending on the spacing of the base stitches and the thickness of thread used for the weaving.

Use a crewel needle for the base stitches and then change to a tapestry needle for the weaving, as it is less likely to catch the fabric as you slide it through.

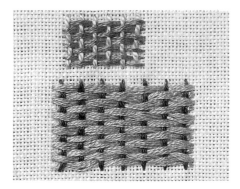

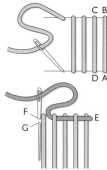

NEEDLE-WEAVING

(Queen Anne stitch)

1. Bring a crewel needle to the front at A and insert it at B. Bring it up at C and insert it at D, continuing across the area.

2. Using a tapestry needle, bring a second thread to the front at the top right, at E, and take it over the first straight stitch and under the second. Weave across the area, taking care not to catch the fabric.

3. At the end of the row, insert the needle at F and bring it out just below, at G. Weave back, going over the stitches that were passed under and vice versa.

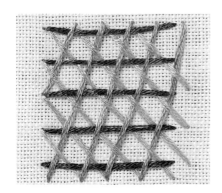

HONEYCOMB FILLING

This stitch is usually worked in three color values. Use a hoop to hold the fabric taut and mark a regular grid on plainweave fabrics (see p.109).

1. Bring the first-color thread to the front of the fabric at the top left and make a series of evenly spaced horizontal straight stitches across the area, as shown in the top diagram.

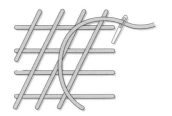

2. Bring the second-color thread to the front and make a series of parallel diagonal stitches across the area, bringing the needle out at the bottom and inserting it at the top.

3. Bring the third-color thread to the front at the top left, at A, and weave the thread over and under the first two threads. Insert the needle at B and bring it out at C, as shown in the bottom diagram.

4. Continue across the area.

HELPFUL HINT

Woven filling stitches can be worked entirely in one color for a subtle, textured effect. Working in several colors does, however, showcase the woven pattern better.

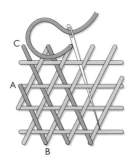

TWISTED LATTICE FILLING

This stitch is used for filling areas with a slightly raised, lattice design. A second sequence of weaving may be done after the first is finished, for a less open look. Use a hoop to hold the fabric taut and mark a regular grid on plainweave fabrics (see p. 109). Use a tapestry needle for weaving.

1. Bring a crewel needle to the front of the fabric at A and insert it at B, as shown in the top diagram. Bring it up at C and continue making diagonal stitches over the area.

2. Starting at the top left-hand edge, at D, work diagonal stitches back the other way, but weave them over and under the existing diagonals, taking care not to catch the fabric, as shown.

3. Bring a new color of thread to the front at E, beside the top left-hand intersection. Take it over the intersection and slide it under the lower diagonal from right to left, taking care not to catch the fabric.

4. Now take it over the lower intersection and slide it under the upper diagonal from right to left and continue along the row, as shown in the bottom diagram.

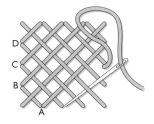

5. At the end of the row, insert the needle beside the last intersection and bring it out at the right end of the next row. Continue weaving backward and forward as required.

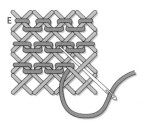

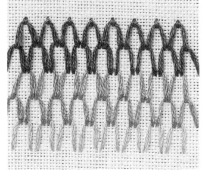

WAVE FILLING

(Looped shading stitch)

On plainweave fabric, mark parallel lines (see p. 53).

1. Bring a crewel needle to the front at the top left, at A. Insert it at B and out at C. Continue to make short stitches (see upper diagram).

2. Using a tapestry needle, bring the thread out at D. Take it up and slide the needle under the first stitch, taking care not to catch the fabric. Insert the needle at E and bring it out at F. Continue to the end of the row.

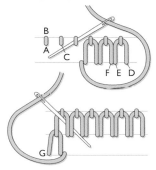

3. Bring the needle up at G and slide it under the end vertical. Insert it beside G, the space being the same size as E–D, and out again, and then continue to the right, sliding it under two verticals of the row above (see lower diagram). Work backward and forward across the area in the same way.

CLOUD FILLING

On plainweave fabric, mark parallel lines for each line of stitching (see p. 53).

1. Bring a crewel needle to the front of the fabric at the top left, at A, and make a row of short vertical stitches across the area. Make additional rows as required, placing those in each row midway between the stitches in the row above.

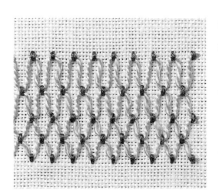

2. Using a tapestry needle, bring the thread up under the stitch at B and slide it under the first stitch of the second row, taking care not to catch the fabric. Then slide it under the next stitch on the first row and continue to the end of the row. Insert the needle under the stitch at A and bring it out under the first stitch of the third row.

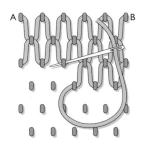

3. Continue to the right and insert the needle under the last stitch. Bring it out close by and continue as before.

CEYLON *stitch*

(Peruvian knitting, knitting stitch)

This stitch is used as a broad band or filling for smaller areas. On evenweave fabric, work over a consistent number of threads; on plainweave fabric mark regularly spaced dots down the edges (see p. 53). For the best results, use an embroidery hoop or frame. Work from top to bottom.

1. Bring a crewel needle to the front of the fabric at the top left dot, at A, and insert it at the top right dot. Make a series of short anchoring stitches across it, working from right to left (see diagram 1).

2. Using a tapestry needle, bring the thread out at B. Loop the thread around to the right and slide the needle under the top thread from top to bottom, with the working thread under the needle and taking care not to catch the fabric (see diagram 2). Keep the loops fairly loose.

3. Make similar loops across to the right and insert the needle at the right end of the row (see diagram 3).

4. Bring the needle out at C and slide the needle from right to left under both threads of the loops above. At the end of the row, insert the needle into the fabric (see diagram 4). Add and subtract stitches on the edges to widen or narrow the area to be covered.

5. Continue rows as required. To finish, make a small vertical stitch over each loop of the last row.

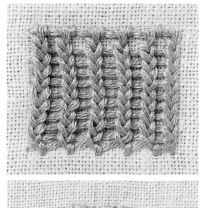

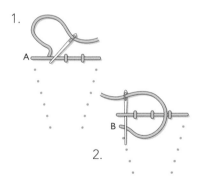

1.

2.

3.

4.

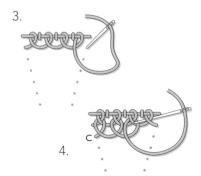

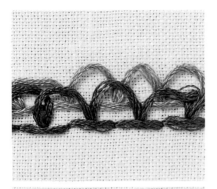

TURKEY WORK

(Ghiordes knot, single-knot tufting)

This stitch makes a soft pile and is often used in wool embroidery. On plainweave fabric, mark closely spaced parallel lines of regular dots (see p. 53). Work from left to right.

1. Begin with the needle on the front of the fabric and take it to the back at A. Pull the thread through to leave a tail (see diagram 1).

2. Bring the needle out at B and insert it at C (see diagram 2). Then bring it out at A, taking care not to catch the back stitch.

3. Insert the needle at D (see diagram 3), and pull the thread through. Leave a loop the length of the tail.

4. Bring the needle up at C and put it in at E. Bring it out at D to form the second loop. Continue in the same way, ending with a back stitch.

5. Work the second row and later rows from left to right in the same way (see diagram 4).

6. To finish, cut the loops and trim them to the required height.

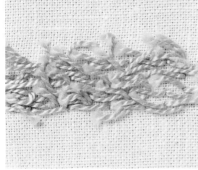

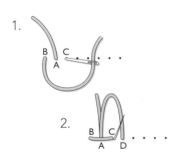

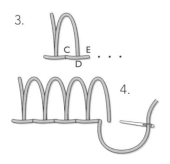

insertion stitches

Insertion stitches are used to join two pieces of fabric with an open, decorative band. They are forms of buttonhole and herringbone stitches. When choosing one for a particular piece of embroidery, consider whether a strong join is required or whether it serves a purely decorative function.

Hem both pieces of fabric before you start and baste them to a sheet of clean, strong paper to keep them in place while you stitch. Use a crewel needle for the embroidery.

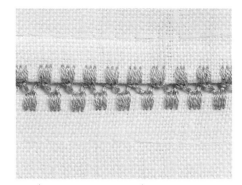

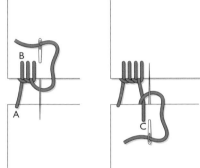

BUTTONHOLE INSERTION *stitch*

(Blanket insertion stitch)

This stitch gives a strong join. Work from left to right.

1. Bring a crewel needle to the front at the left-hand end of the lower piece of fabric, at A. Insert it at B on the upper piece and work the first group of buttonhole stitches (p. 81). Two, three, or four stitches are usual.

2. Bring the needle up at C on the lower piece and work the next group of buttonhole stitches upside down.

HERRINGBONE INSERTION *stitch*

(Faggoting)

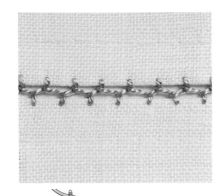

This stitch makes a lacy join. Work from left to right or top to bottom.

1. Bring a crewel needle to the front from inside the folded hem of the lower piece of fabric at A, as shown in the top diagram.

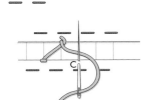

2. Insert the needle at B on the upper piece and pull through with the thread under the needle, as shown.

3. Insert the needle in on the lower piece at C and pull through with the thread under the needle, as shown in the lower diagram.

4. Continue as required.

TWISTED INSERTION *stitch*

(Twisted faggot stitch, twisted herringbone insertion)

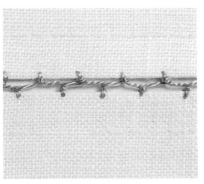

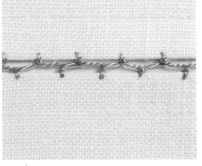

This stitch makes a decorative join between two pieces of fabric. Work from left to right.

1. Bring a crewel needle to the front from inside the folded hem of the lower piece of fabric at A.

2. Insert the needle into the upper piece from the back, at B, and pull the thread through.

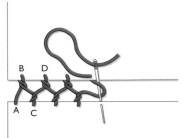

3. Twist the needle in the thread once and insert it into the lower piece from the back at C, as shown at left. Then twist the needle in the thread and put it into the upper piece from the back, at D, as shown.

4. Continue as required.

KNOTTED
INSERTION *stitch*

(Knotted faggot stitch, knotted herringbone insertion)

This stitch makes a strong, decorative join between two pieces of fabric. Work from left to right.

1. Bring a crewel needle to the front from inside the folded hem of the lower piece of fabric at A, as shown in the upper diagram.

2. Insert the needle into the upper piece at B and pull the thread to the right, making a loop. Slip the needle under both threads, from left to right, bringing it out within the loop of the thread, and pull through to make a knot.

3. Insert the needle into the lower piece at C and repeat, as shown in the lower diagram.

HELPFUL HINT

Always choose an insertion stitch that gives a strong join for table or bed linen that will require regular washing.

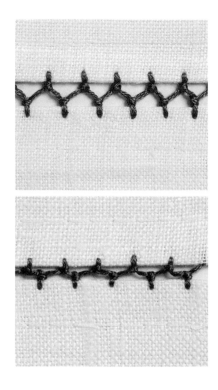

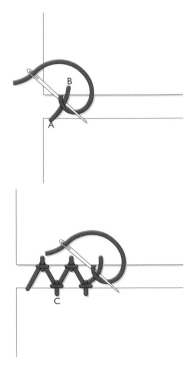

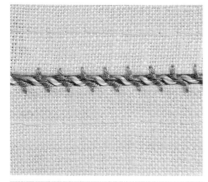

LACED INSERTION
stitch

(Laced faggot stitch)

This stitch makes a strong, decorative join between two pieces of fabric. Hem nonselvage edges, but do not tack the fabric pieces to the paper at first. Work from right to left.

1. Bring a crewel needle to the front from inside the folded hem of the lower piece of fabric at A.

2. Twist the thread around the needle once and insert the needle from the back at B. With the thread turned back under the needle, pull the thread through, as shown in the upper diagram.

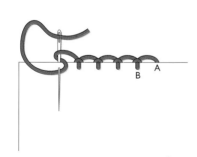

3. Continue stitching along the edge of the lower fabric. Repeat on the upper piece of fabric, starting with a short stitch so that the loops on the two pieces are staggered.

4. Tack the pieces to paper an appropriate distance apart. Using a tapestry needle, bring the thread to the front at C and lace back and forth through the loops (as shown in the lower diagram).

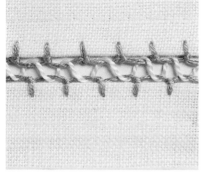

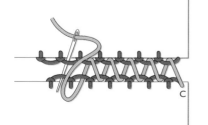

ITALIAN INSERTION
stitch
(Italian faggot stitch)

This stitch makes a wide decorative join between two pieces of fabric. More buttonhole stitches can be worked for a wider gap, fewer for a smaller one. Hem non-selvedge edges and tack the pieces of fabric to paper. Work from top to bottom.

1. Bring a crewel needle to the front of the right-hand fabric at A and put it through the second piece of fabric at B, as shown in diagram 1.

2. Stitch four buttonhole stitches (p. 81) over the thread, starting at the left, as shown in diagram 2.

3. Insert the needle through the right-hand fabric at C and pull through with the thread under the needle. Repeat at D on the other piece, as shown in diagram 3.

4. Beginning at C, work four buttonhole stitches over the two threads. Then insert the needle through the fabric at E and pull through with the thread under the needle as before.

5. Beginning at D, work four buttonhole stitches over both threads, as shown in diagram 4.

6. Continue as required.

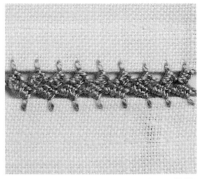

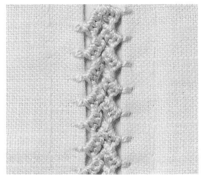

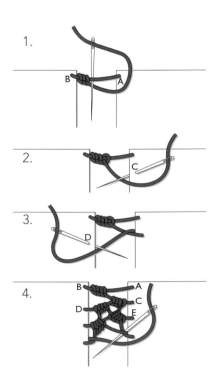

drawn-thread stitches

Drawn-thread stitches are used on embroidery when horizontal threads have been pulled to create an openwork band. The stitches secure the edges of the band and group the vertical threads into patterns.

These stitches are worked on evenweave fabrics *only*, using a tapestry needle. The thread chosen should be strong and the same weight as the threads in the fabric. Begin with a small back stitch to secure the thread.

Pulling the threads

1. Determine the area of the drawn-thread band, allowing for a hem, if required.

2. Baste around the area of the openwork band, placing the basting stitches between the fabric threads. Also mark the center of the band with basting stitches.

3. At the center, cut through the horizontal threads with small, sharp scissors.

4. Using a tapestry needle, unweave the cut threads back toward the sides. Make sure that the number of vertical threads you expose will divide evenly into the number of pattern bundles you desire.

5. Secure the cut threads by weaving them back into the sides over about six threads.

6. If a hem is required, iron and baste it in place.

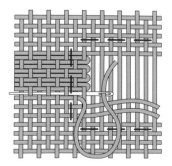

HEM *stitch*

(Spoke stitch)

This stitch is used to make a hem or simply to group vertical threads in an open band together. It can be worked from front or back, but is traditionally worked from the back when used with a hem. Baste the hem in place. Use a tapestry needle and work from left to right.

1. Count the vertical threads. The number of threads in each bundle you wrap together must be the same, so make sure the number you choose (three, four, or five) will divide evenly into the vertical threads available.

2. With the wrong side of the work facing upward, take the needle between the two layers of fabric at A, at the left-hand end, and make a small back stitch to hold the thread securely, as shown in the upper diagram.

3. Take the needle under the first bundle of threads from right to left and pull them together.

4. Insert the needle in to the right of this bundle at B so that it catches the top of the hem and comes out facing you, as shown in the lower diagram.

5. Continue as required.

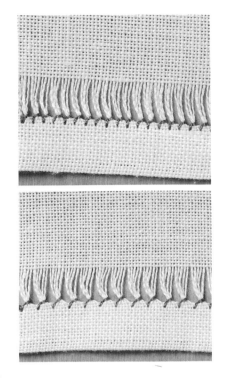

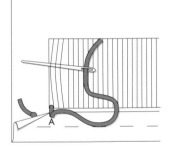

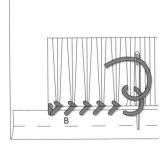

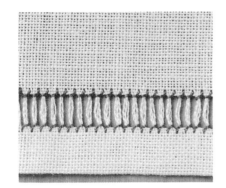

LADDER HEM *stitch*

(Ladder stitch)

This stitch is used to hem both sides of a drawn-thread border. Use a tapestry needle and work from left to right.

1. Work the hem stitch (see diagram at left) along one side of the border.

2. Turn the piece around and work hem stitch along the other side, as shown in the diagram.

3. If there is a corner, stitch one side of the outside edge first and finish off the thread before turning the corner and starting again. On the inside edge, take the thread around the last bundle on one side and then immediately around the first bundle on the next side without stitching into the fabric.

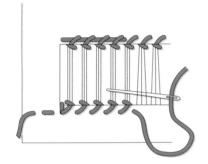

SERPENTINE HEM *stitch*

(Zigzag hem stitch, trellis hem stitch)

This stitch is used for a drawn-thread border. Each bundle must contain an even number of threads so that it can be split in two. Use a tapestry needle and work from left to right.

1. Work the hem stitch (see diagram at left) along one side of the border.

2. Turn the piece around and work hem stitch along the other side, starting with a half bundle.

3. Continue as required, finishing with another half bundle.

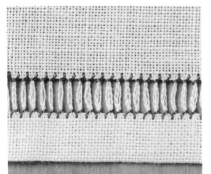

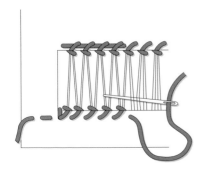

DOUBLE HEM *stitch*

This stitch is used for a decorative drawn-thread border. Withdraw two bands of threads and leave four to six threads in the middle. Use a tapestry needle and work from right to left.

1. Secure the thread at the right-hand end, beside the top of the lower band.

2. Take the needle under and then over the first bundle of the lower band, as shown in the diagram.

3. Take the needle under the middle fabric band and bring it out to the left of the first bundle in the upper band.

4. Take the needle over and under this bundle, and then over the fabric band to bring it out to the left of the second bundle on the lower band. Continue as required.

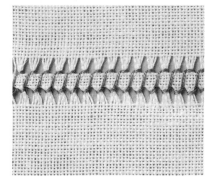

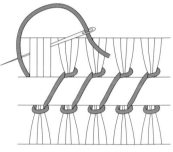

INTERLACED HEM *stitch*

(Twisted border, crossing cluster border)

This stitch can be worked over and under one or two bundles. Use a tapestry needle. Work from left to right.

1. Work the hem stitch (p. 144) along one side of the border. Turn the piece around and work the hem stitch along the other side.

2. Turn the fabric so that the right side is facing you. Secure the thread with waste back stitches at the right-hand end, midway between the two rows of hem stitch, as shown in the upper diagram.

3. Take the thread over the first and second bundles; then slide the needle under the second bundle from left to right. With the tip of the needle, pull the first bundle under the second and then pull the thread through. Continue as required.

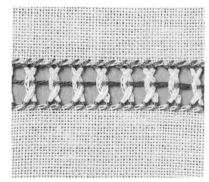

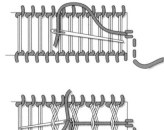

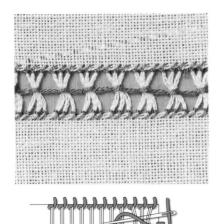

KNOTTED BORDER
stitch

(Knotted clusters)

1. Using a tapestry needle, work the ladder hem stitch (p. 145) along the border, making sure that the number of bundles is divisible by the number of vertical threads you want to group together.

2. Turn the fabric so that the right side is facing you. Secure the thread with waste back stitches at the right-hand end, midway between the two rows of hem stitch, as shown in the upper diagram.

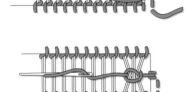

3. Loop the thread over the first group of bundles and take the needle under the group from right to left. Bring it out within the loop of thread, as shown in the lower diagram. Pull the thread tight and continue as required.

DOUBLE-KNOTTED BORDER *stitch*

(Double cluster border)

1. Work the ladder hem stitch (p. 145) along the border, making sure that the number of bundles is divisible by four.

2. Turn the fabric so the right side is facing you. Secure the thread with waste back stitches at the right-hand end, a third of the way up from the bottom of the border.

3. Loop the thread over the first four bundles and take the needle under them from right to left. Bring it out within the loop of thread, pull tight, and continue to the end of the border, as shown in the diagram.

4. Secure the thread at the right-hand end. Knot together the first two bundles and then work over four at a time to the end. Knot the last two bundles and finish off.

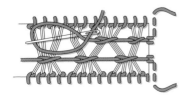

OVERCAST BAR

(Corded cluster)

1. Count the vertical threads. The number in each bundle must be the same (three, four, or five is usual).

2. With right side facing, work from right to left. Bringing the needle to the front of the fabric, bottom right, take it under the top of the first bundle from right to left, holding the end of the working thread along the bundle.

3. Pass the needle under the bundle from right to left again, covering the working thread and the bundle. Continue, pulling the working thread firmly and arranging the threads neatly and close together until the bundle is covered. Take the thread to the top of the next bundle.

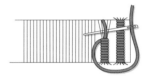

4. Cover the next bundle from bottom to top, continuing up and down until all bundles are covered.

ZIGZAG OVERCAST BAR

This stitch is used for wide drawn-thread borders. Use a tapestry needle and work from right to left.

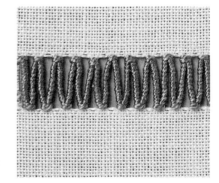

1. Count the vertical threads. The number of threads in each bundle must be the same, so make sure that the number you choose (three, four, or five) will divide evenly into the number of vertical threads available.

2. Work one overcast bar (see diagram) from top to bottom.

3. Wrap the thread twice around the base of the wrapped bar and the next bundle together. Keep the thread taut.

4. Wrap the second bundle from bottom to top, and then wrap the thread twice around the top of both the wrapped bar and the next bundle. Continue as required.

WOVEN BAR

(Needleweaving cluster, darned bars)

Use a tapestry needle and work from right to left.

1. Count the vertical threads. The number in each bundle must be the same and must be an even number.

2. With the right side of the fabric facing you, hold the thread along the first bundle. Take the needle under the right-hand half of the bundle from right to left, bringing it up in the center (see upper diagram).

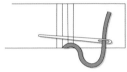

3. Take the needle under the left-hand half of the bundle from left to right, bringing it up in the center (see lower diagram).

4. Continue until the bundle is covered. Arrange the stitches with the tip of the needle and don't overpack the vertical threads.

WOVEN BAR WITH PICOT

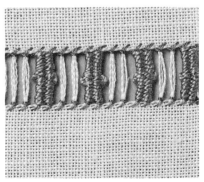

1. Count the vertical threads. The number in each bundle must be the same and must be an even number.

2. With the right side of the fabric facing you and working from right to left, hold the thread along the first bundle. Take the needle under the right half of the bundle from right to left, bringing it up in the center.

3. Take the needle under the left half of the bundle from left to right, bringing it up in the center (see diagram).

4. Continue until the bundle is half covered. Loop the thread over the bundle and pass the needle under the right-hand half, bringing it up within the loop. Pull the thread firmly.

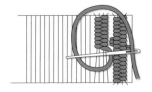

5. Repeat on the left-hand side. Finish the bar as usual.

BUTTONHOLE CORNER WITH LOOP *stitch*

This stitch is used to fill a corner in a drawn-thread border. Use a tapestry needle.

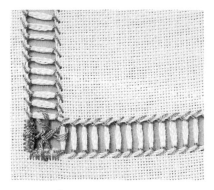

1. With the right side of the fabric facing you, make a waste knot (p. 22) at the left-hand end of the corner.

2. Work buttonhole stitches (p. 81) along the two outside edges of the corner, making one stitch between each two threads. The stitches should be close together and two or three threads deep.

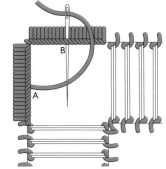

3. Take the thread along the back of the stitches and bring it out through the buttonhole stitch at the center of the left-hand side at A.

4. With the thread under the needle, insert the needle into the buttonhole stitch at the center of the top at B, as shown in the upper diagram.

5. Again, with the thread under the needle, take the needle under a bundle at C and then repeat at D, as shown at right.

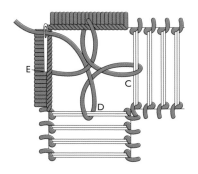

6. Insert the needle at E through the buttonhole stitch and finish off, as shown in the lower diagram.

HELPFUL HINT

If a thread breaks as it is being pulled out, remove the first part and smooth the fabric. Use a pin to pick up the broken end and continue.

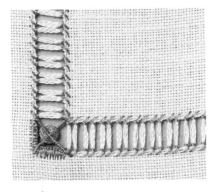

DOVE'S EYE CORNER

This stitch is used to fill and strengthen a corner in a drawn-thread border. Use a tapestry needle.

1. With the right side of the fabric facing you, make a waste knot (p. 22) at the left-hand end of the corner.

2. Work buttonhole stitches (p. 81) along the two outside edges of the corner, making one stitch between each two threads. The stitches should be close together and two or three threads deep.

3. Take the thread along the back of the stitches and bring it out at the lower left at A, as shown in the upper diagram.

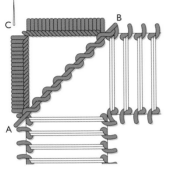

4. Insert the needle in at B and overcast (p. 148) the thread back to A. Insert the needle at A, as shown.

5. Slide the needle under the buttonhole stitch and bring it out at C. Insert it at D and overcast the thread back to the center, as shown in the middle diagram.

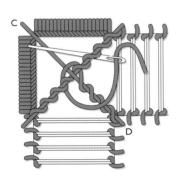

6. Take the needle under the top right thread and weave over and under as required. Then overcast back to C, as shown in the lower diagram.

7. Insert the needle at C and finish off.

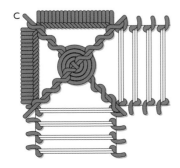

SPIDER WEB CORNER

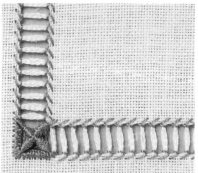

This stitch is used to fill and strengthen a corner in a drawn-thread border. Use a tapestry needle.

1. With the right side of the fabric facing you, make a waste knot (p. 22) at the left-hand end of the corner.

2. Work buttonhole stitches (p. 81) along the two outside edges of the corner, making one stitch between each two threads. The stitches should be close together and two or three threads deep.

3. Take the thread along the back of the stitches and bring it out at the outside corner at A.

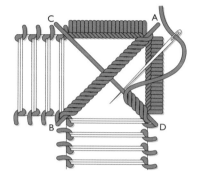

4. Insert the needle at B and overcast (p. 148) the thread back to A. Insert the needle at A.

5. Slide the needle under the buttonhole stitch and bring it out at C. Take it under the overcast bar and insert it at D, as shown on the upper diagram. Overcast the thread back to the center.

6. Work a spider's web in an counterclockwise direction by sliding the needle under the top-right spoke and then bring it back and slide it under the same spoke and the top-left one. Take care not to catch the fabric, as shown in the lower diagram.

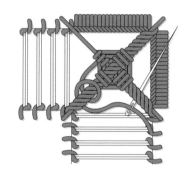

7. Bring the needle back and pass it under the top-left and bottom-left spokes, continuing as required.

8. To finish, overcast the visible part of the top left spoke.

WHEEL CORNER

This stitch is used with the interlaced hem stitch to fill and strengthen the corner. Use a tapestry needle.

1. Work the interlaced hem stitch (p. 146) along the borders, securing the threads so they cross at the corners.

2. With the right side of the fabric facing you, make a waste knot (p. 22) at the left-hand end of the corner.

3. Work buttonhole stitches (p. 81) along the two outside edges of the corner, making one stitch between each two threads. The stitches should be close together and two or three threads deep.

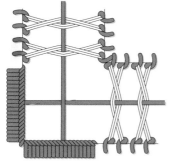

4. Take the thread along the back of the stitches and bring it out at the lower left at A, as shown in the top diagram.

5. Insert the needle in at B and overcast (p. 148) the thread back to the center. Take the needle under the three threads and then put it in at C.

6. Overcast the thread from C back to the center. Insert the needle above the first overcast thread and bring it out at D, as shown in the middle diagram.

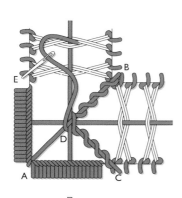

7. Insert the needle at E and overcast the thread back to the center.

8. Take the needle over the center-top thread and then under it and the next thread, in an counterclockwise direction, as shown in the bottom diagram. Continue until all of the spokes are filled.

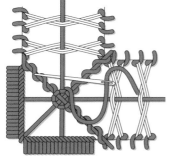

pulled stitches

These stitches are worked on evenweave fabric only, pulling the fabric threads together in groups to create small holes that give texture to the embroidery. The result is usually delicate and precise. Most stitches are used to make filling patterns.

A strong thread is required to withstand the tension, and it should be the same weight as the fabric threads. Keep the tension firm and consistent throughout for an even result and use a tapestry needle.

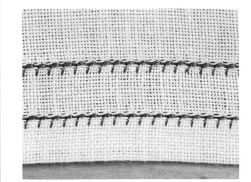

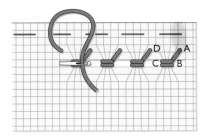

PIN *stitch*
(Point de paris)

This stitch is used to make a hem. Use a tapestry needle and work from right to left over a consistent number of threads. Pull the thread firmly.

1. Baste the hem in place. Turn the fabric so the right side is facing you and the hem is at the top.

2. Bring the needle through the hem to the front of the fabric at A. Insert the needle at B and bring it out at C. Repeat.

3. Insert the needle at B and bring it out at D. Continue as required, keeping the thread taut.

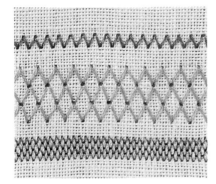

WAVE *stitch*

This stitch is used for borders or filling on evenweave fabric. Use a tapestry needle and work over a consistent number of threads in each direction. Pull the thread firmly to create the holes.

1. Bring the needle to the front of the fabric at A, near the top right of the area.

2. Insert the needle diagonally at the top right at B. Bring it up at C and insert it at A, so that C–A is the same length and symmetrical with A–B.

3. Bring the needle up at D and continue to the end of the row, as shown at top part of the diagram.

4. Turn the fabric around and work the next row into the same holes, as shown in the lower part of the diagram.

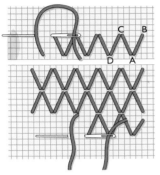

FAGGOT *stitch*

This stitch is used for filling diagonal areas on evenweave fabric. Use a tapestry needle and work over a consistent number of threads (usually four) in each direction. Pull the thread firmly to create the holes.

1. Bring the needle to the front of the fabric at A.

2. Insert the needle at B, four threads to the right of A, and bring it out four threads below and to the right of A, at C.

3. Insert the needle at A and bring it out four threads to the left of C, at D. Then insert the needle in at C and bring it out four threads below D, as shown.

4. Continue down the area and then turn the fabric and repeat, placing the stitches into the same holes as the first row.

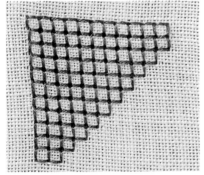

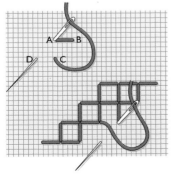

RINGED BACK *stitch*

This stitch is used for borders or filling on evenweave fabric. Use a tapestry needle and work over a consistent number of threads in each direction. Pull the thread through firmly at each stitch to form the holes and work from right to left.

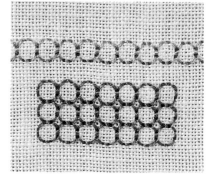

1. Bring the needle to the front of the fabric at A and insert it at B. Then bring it out at C and insert it at A, out at D and in at C.

2. Continue working back stitches to form opposed semicircles, as shown in the top part of the diagram.

3. At the end of the row, turn the fabric around and repeat to the end of the row, placing a second stitch into the same holes where the circles overlap.

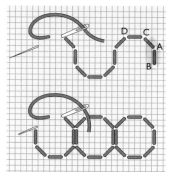

PULLED HONEYCOMB *stitch*

(Pulled brick stitch)

This stitch is used for borders or filling on evenweave fabric. Use a tapestry needle and work over a consistent number of threads in each direction. Pull the thread through firmly at each stitch to form the holes and work from top to bottom.

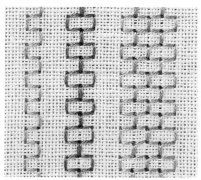

1. Bring the needle to the front of the fabric at A, at top right, and insert it at B. Bring it out at C and put it in at A, then out at D and in at C. Repeat as mirror image.

2. Continue working back stitches to the end of the row, as shown in the diagram.

3. Turn the fabric around and repeat, placing a second vertical stitch into the same holes as in the previous row.

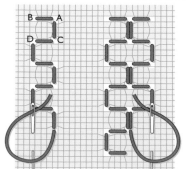

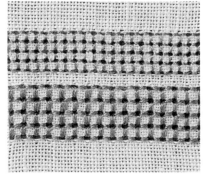

PUNCH *stitch*

This stitch is used for filling on evenweave fabric. Use a tapestry needle and work over a consistent number of threads in each direction, from top right to bottom left, pulling the thread firmly to form the holes.

1. Bring the needle to the front of the fabric at A and insert it at B. Repeat.

2. Bring the needle out at C, insert it at D, and repeat. Continue making double stitches to the end of the row, as shown.

3. Work the second row from left to right and the third from right to left, using the same holes as for the previous row. Continue as required.

4. Turn the fabric and work the other sides of the squares in the same way, stitching into the same holes.

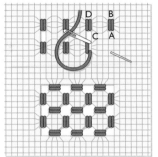

COIL *stitch*

This stitch is used for filling on evenweave fabric. Work over a consistent number of threads and leave an even number between each triple stitch so the rows can be staggered neatly. Use a tapestry needle and work from top right to bottom left, pulling the thread firmly to make the holes.

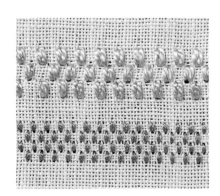

1. Bring the needle to the front of the fabric at A and insert it at B to make the first triple stitch. Repeat twice.

2. Bring the needle out at C and insert it at D to make the next triple stitch. Continue to the end of the row.

3. Work the next row from left to right, placing the stitches midway between those of the first row, as shown.

4. Continue stitching rows as required.

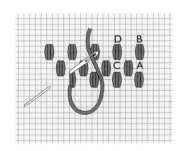

SMOCKING

In this chapter the techniques and stitches used for smocking are described. Although smocking is worked on fabric, it is the specific stitches used to join the gathers that sets this stitch apart from other fabric embroidery.

SMOCKING TECHNIQUES

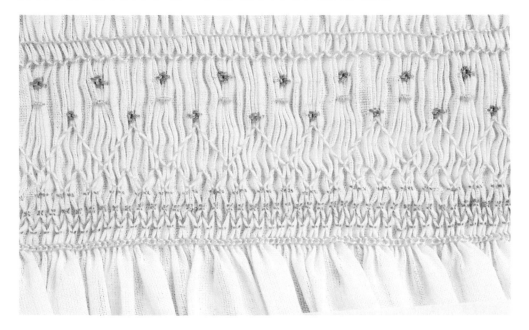

Smocking is ornamental stitching used to gather fabric so that garments can be made without fastenings, since the smocked area can be stretched. It is suitable for yokes, bodices, and cuffs. The technique has been known since early medieval times, but it became especially popular in the seventeenth and eighteenth centuries. It was traditionally used for farmworkers' smocks (these were loose, outer garments worn to protect their clothes), hence its name.

Today smocking is used primarily for babies' and children's clothes and lingerie, but it can also be used on other items purely for its decorative effect.

Materials

Lightweight cotton and silk fabrics are most often chosen for smocking because the fabric must gather easily. Lawns and voiles are generally used. The weave of the fabric must also be stable so that the design is not distorted. Knit fabrics are, therefore, not suitable. Smocking can be worked on fabrics with small, regular patterns, but it will not look well on large or bold prints.

Most embroidery cottons and silk threads can be used. Only one or two strands are needed on fine fabrics, though three or more may be used on heavier ones. Smocking is worked with a crewel needle.

Gathering

Before beginning the embroidery, the fabric must be gathered. This will reduce the width of the piece, so begin with a piece three times as wide as the finished item. Always wash the fabric first to ensure that it will not shrink, and work a test piece so that you know how much "give" the fabric and thread will have and how the gathers will look. Leave at least 1 in. (2.5 cm) all around the smocked area and oversew or bind the edges to prevent fraying.

Traditional method

1. On the wrong side of the fabric, mark a grid of dots, aligning them with the straight grain of the fabric. To do this, place dressmaker's carbon paper on the fabric and a sheet of graph paper over it. Press a ballpoint pen against the intersections. Dots are usually ⅛–¼ in. (3–6 mm) apart. If preferred, sheets of smocking dots can be purchased and ironed onto the fabric. Follow the manufacturer's instructions carefully so that they do not smudge.

2. Flatten out the fabric. Using sewing thread in a color that contrasts with the fabric, make running stitches (p.47) across each row of dots, picking up a few threads at each dot. You can start each row of stitches with a knot, or tie the ends together in pairs. Leave a tail of thread at the end of each row, as shown at right.

3. Gather the fabric a little smaller than the

Iron sheets of smocking dots onto the fabric.

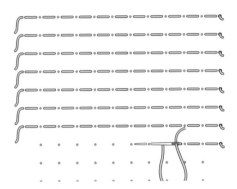

Pick up a few threads at each dot.

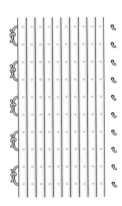

Gather the fabric firmly but not too tightly.

required width—it will expand slightly when the gathering threads are removed—and tie off the ends of the threads in pairs. The gathering should be firm but not tight. Adjust the gathers evenly.

4. Remove the gathering threads after the smocking is completed.

Alternative methods

Smocking can also be worked on fabrics with small, regular patterns such as checks, dots, or tiny flowers without the need for dots. The fabric pattern is used as a guide for the gathering.

"Mock" smocking, in which the dots are marked on the right side of the fabric and the smocking is worked without prior gathering, is also becoming more common.

General guidelines for smocking

- Mark the center of the gathered area at top and bottom as a guide for later positioning of the garment pattern.
- Work on the right side of the fabric, along a row of gathering stitches and from left to right.
- Always anchor the thread firmly at the beginning of a row, using a double back stitch (p.29) or a smocker's knot (p. 165).
- At each stitch pick up only the top third of the pleat and always keep the needle horizontal. Pick up only one pleat at a time.
- Make each stitch either above the gathering thread or below it. Never make a stitch across it because the embroidery will be distorted or damaged when you

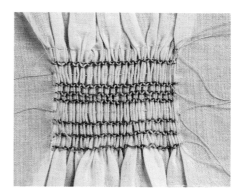

The gathering stitches are removed after the smocking has been embroidered.

remove the gathering threads.

- Before you begin the design, work a row of cable stitch (see photographs on p.163) along the top and bottom of the area to be smocked, to control the work. These rows can become part of the design or can be removed once the smocking is complete. They can be worked on the wrong side of the work if desired.
- If the smocking design is widely spaced and does not hold the pleats evenly in place, rows of cable stitch (p.163) may be stitched on the wrong side (back smocking) to improve elasticity. They may be added before or after smocking the design and are usually worked just below each row of gathering stitches, using two strands of cotton floss.
- Pull the thread through firmly at each stitch to maintain the tension. If you pull too tightly, the work will lack elasticity.

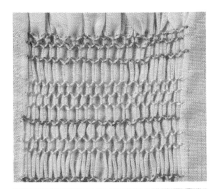

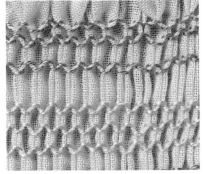

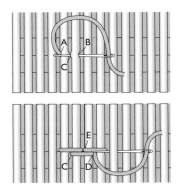

CABLE *stitch*

(Alternate stem stitch)

This stitch is the basic smocking stitch. It is used to make single or multiple lines. Work on the right side of the fabric, along a row of gathering stitch and from left to right.

1. Bring a crewel needle to the front of the fabric at A, at the left-hand edge of the first gather to be worked.

2. With the thread above the needle, take the needle across two gathers and take a small stitch backward from B to C, so that C is lower than A–B. This is an "over cable" (see upper diagram).

3. Then take the needle over two gathers and take a similar stitch from D to E, but with the thread below the needle and so that E is above C–D. This is an "under cable" (see lower diagram). Continue alternating over and under cables to the end of the row. Finish with a double back stitch (p.29).

4. Additional rows can be worked as required, either consistently spaced or in groups. Each row can be the same as the first, or each second row can be a mirror image of the first to build up blocks of stitches.

STEM *stitch*

(Rope stitch)

1. Bring the needle to the front of the fabric at A, at the left-hand edge of the first gather, as shown in the diagram below.

2. Looping the thread around below the needle, take the needle across two gathers and take a small stitch backward from B to C, so that C is higher than A–B.

3. Continue to the end of the row and finish with a double back stitch (p.29). Work additional rows as required.

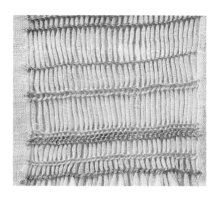

Mock chain stitch

This stitch consists of a row of stem stitch (p.48) with a row of outline stitch (p. 50) immediately below it (see the center line in the photograph).

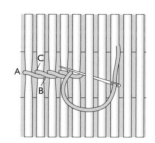

OUTLINE *stitch*

This stitch is worked in the same way as stem stitch but with the thread above the needle, so the stitches slope the opposite way.

1. Bring a crewel needle to the front of the fabric at A, at the left-hand edge of the first gather.

2. Looping the thread around above the needle, take the needle across two gathers and take a small stitch backward from B to C, so that C is lower than A–B, as shown in the diagram.

3. Continue to the end of the row and finish with a double back stitch (p.29).

4. Work additional rows as required.

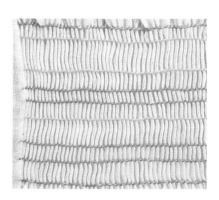

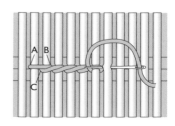

SMOCKER'S KNOT

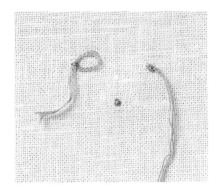

This stitch makes a firm knot to finish off smocking or other embroidery, and it can also be used for decoration.

1. Using a crewel needle, Make a small back stitch from B to A, but do not pull through completely. Leave a small loop.

2. Pass the needle through the loop and pull through to leave a second small loop, as shown.

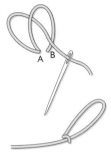

3. Take the thread in your left hand and pull the second loop with your right hand until the first loop is tight.

4. Pass the needle through the second loop and pull through to form a firm knot. Insert the needle under the knot.

CABLE FLOWERETTE

1. Bring a crewel needle to the front of the fabric at A, at the left-hand edge of the first gather.

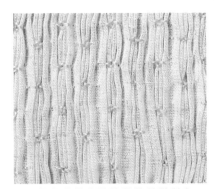

2. With the thread below the needle, take the needle across two gathers and take a small stitch backward from B to C, so that C is higher than A–B, as shown.

3. With the thread above the needle, take the needle across two gathers to D and back through one to B.

4. With the thread again above the needle, take the needle across two gathers to E and back through three gathers to come up at F, below A–B.

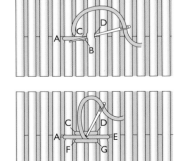

5. With the thread below the needle, take the needle across two gathers to G and come up again at B. Take the needle down over a couple of threads to finish off.

WAVE *stitch*

(Chevron stitch, diamond stitch)

1. Bring a crewel needle to the front of the fabric at A, at the left-hand edge of the first gather on the lower gathering line.

2. With the thread below the needle, take it across two gathers. Insert the needle at B and bring it out between the gathers at C, as shown in the top diagram.

3. On the upper gathering line, take the needle through the third gather from right to left (D to E). Keep the thread below the needle.

4. Still on the upper line but with the thread now above the needle, take a stitch across the fourth gather from F to D. Then return to the lower line and take a stitch across the fifth gather, as shown in the middle diagram.

5. Repeat to the end of the row. Work the next row again from the left, keeping the thread below the needle when working upward and above it when working downward, as shown in the bottom diagram. The second row may be worked in the same way as the first or as a mirror image.

HELPFUL HINT

If you use printed fabric for smocking, make sure the print is straight on the fabric grain, or the embroidery will appear to be crooked. Be careful, too, to choose a print that will not overpower the embroidery.

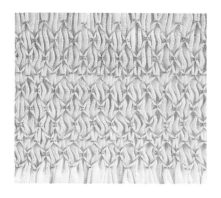

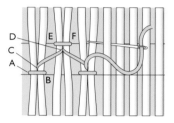

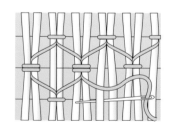

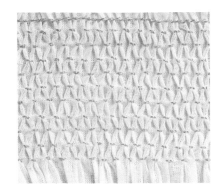

HONEYCOMB *stitch*

1. Bring the needle to the front of the fabric at A, at the left-hand edge of the first gather on the upper line.

2. Take a crewel needle across two gathers and take a small stitch backward from B to A. Then again insert the needle at B and bring it out on the lower line beside the second gather at C, as shown in the diagram.

3. Take the needle across two gathers and take a small stitch backward from D to C. Then again insert the needle at D and bring it out on the upper line beside the third gather at E.

4. Continue in the same way. Finish with a double back stitch (p. 29).

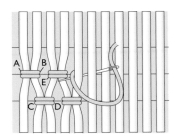

SURFACE HONEYCOMB *stitch*

(Vandyke stitch)

1. Bring a crewel needle to the front of the fabric at A, at the left edge of the first gather on the upper line. Take the needle across two gathers and insert the needle at B. Bring it out between the gathers at C.

2. Insert the needle at D, between the second and third gathers and just above the lower line, and bring it out at E, at the left of the second gather and on the lower line, as shown in the diagram.

3. Insert the needle at F and bring it out at D. Then insert it at G, between the third and fourth gathers and near the upper line, bringing it out at H.

4. Continue to the end of the row, finishing with a double back stitch (p. 29).

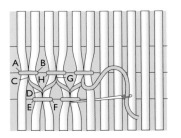

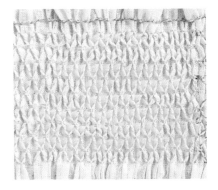

TRELLIS *stitch*

(Chevron stitch, Vandyke stitch, wave stitch)

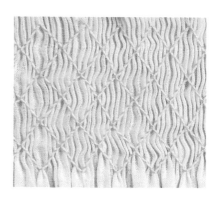

1. Bring a crewel needle to the front of the fabric at A, at the left edge of the first gather on the fourth gathering line.

2. With the thread below the needle, take it across two gathers. Insert the needle at B and bring it out between the gathers at C.

3. On the next gathering line up, take the needle through the third gather from right to left (D to E). Keep the thread below the needle. Repeat on the next gathering line and the fourth gather from F to G, and on the top gathering line and fifth gather, from H to I (see upper diagram).

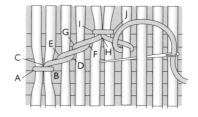

4. Still on the top line but with the thread now above the needle, take a stitch across the sixth gather from J to H. Then work down the other side of the zigzag in the same way, with the thread above the needle.

5. Repeat to the end of the row. Work the next row again from the left, keeping the thread below the needle when working upward and above it when working downward. The second row may be worked in the same way as the first or as a mirror image (see lower diagram).

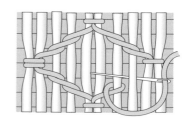

HELPFUL HINT

Always wash the fabric to be smocked before you begin gathering. This removes any chemicals in the fabric and realigns the weave. Very lightweight fabric will be easier to work with if you spray it lightly with starch and iron it.

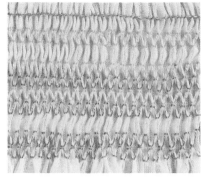

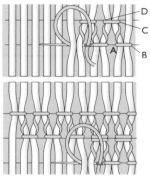

VANDYKE *stitch*

(Surface honeycomb stitch)

1. Bring a crewel needle to the front of the fabric at A, at the right edge of the second gather on the lower line. With the thread below the needle, take it back across the two gathers, insert it at B, and bring it out again at A.

2. On the upper gathering line, take the needle through the second and third gathers from right to left (C to D), and then take it through again (see upper diagram).

3. Return to the lower line and take the needle through the third and fourth gathers, and then again (see lower diagram).

4. Repeat to the end of the row. Work the next row again from the right. The second row may be worked in the same way as the first or as a mirror image.

BULLION *stitch*

This stitch can be used to give additional texture to the smocking. It can be worked over four, five, or six gathers.

1. Bring a crewel needle to the front of the fabric at the top of a gather (A). Loop the thread downward and hold it with your thumb. Take the needle to the right end of the required stitch at B, and put it through the gathers, bringing out the tip just above A (see upper diagram).

2. Take the thread from A up under the needle and wrap it around the needle enough times so that the stitch will extend back to where the needle is inserted (see lower diagram). Arrange the wraps neatly and don't make them too tight.

3. Hold the wraps firmly and push the needle through the fabric and wraps. Pull the thread firmly toward B, keeping the thread taut. Insert the needle at B so that the stitch sits between A and B.

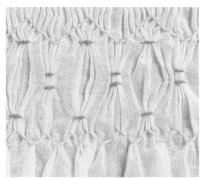

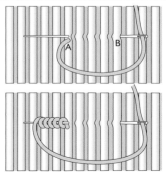

embroidery on CANVAS

This chapter covers the main techniques for canvas work and the stitches used. The canvas on which they are worked provides a regular grid for the stitches.

CANVAS WORK

Canvas work, or needlepoint, goes back at least to the medieval period, when it was known as *opus pulvinarium*, or cushion work. It is strong and hard-wearing, and well suited for use as upholstery and wall hangings. When worked on fine canvas of sixteen or more holes to 1 in. (2.5 cm), it is known as petit point; on canvas of between seven and sixteen holes to 1 in. (2.5 cm) as gros point; and on canvas of less than seven holes to 1 in. (2.5 cm) as quick point. Canvas work is often known as "tapestry" because it originally imitated woven tapestries.

Materials

Canvas is a strong fabric made from hemp, flax, or cotton, and it has an open, regular, weave. It is treated with sizing to stiffen it, and it should be kept dry until the work is completed. Canvas comes in a number of sizes, or gauges, referring to the number of threads per 1 in. (2.5 cm).

There are two main types of canvas.

Single-mesh, or mono, canvas has a grid of single threads and comes in a range of gauges, from 10 to 22. Interlock single-mesh canvas, in which each of the horizontal threads consists of two twisted threads so that the horizontal and vertical threads can be locked together, is stronger than plain woven canvas.

Double-mesh canvas also known as Penelope canvas, has pairs of threads in both directions and comes in gauges from 7 to 10. The secondary grid and smaller holes are useful for fine work.

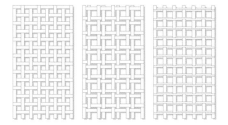

Single-mesh canvas, double-mesh canvas, and interlocked canvas.

Canvas work is often worked with wool yarns, although cottons and silks can also be used, particularly for finer work. Delicate threads may, however, catch on the canvas and be difficult to use. A tapestry needle is used, so as not to split the canvas threads.

Techniques

In canvas work the canvas is usually completely covered by the embroidery, which makes good coverage important. Before you start a project, always work a test piece to make sure that the threads are thick enough for the canvas and

Canvas work is well suited to geometric patterns, such as this elegant star design in tent stitch.

chosen stitches. Oversew or bind the edges of the canvas to prevent fraying.

● The canvas piece should allow for at least a 2-in. (5-cm) margin all around the design.

● Like counted-thread embroidery, canvas work is normally done by working from a chart and counting threads, although sometimes the design is printed or painted onto the canvas. Simple designs can also be drawn directly onto the canvas with a waterproof pen, as the lines will be covered by the embroidery.

- Begin work near the center to make counting threads easier.
- To prevent threads fraying as they are repeatedly pulled through the canvas, use the stab method (see p. 22) of stitching and cut lengths to about 18 in. (45 cm). Begin with a waste knot or waste back stitches (p. 22).
- Work the motifs first, the background last.
- Although it is not essential to use a frame, the finished piece will be less distorted if you do use one, especially when you are working diagonal stitches. Most pieces will be distorted during stitching and will require some blocking (see p. 14) to return them to shape.

Tramming

Tramming is a technique that can be used to increase thread coverage of the canvas. It raises the stitches slightly and makes the embroidery more hard-wearing. Tramming is used on double-mesh canvas when the stitches are worked over both threads.

Bring the needle and thread to the front of the canvas between the double threads at the left end of the row. Put it in at the right end, also between the threads. If the row is long, work a series of long stitches so that each stitch overlaps the last one by one double thread. Work your chosen stitch along the row from right to left, as shown in the diagram top right, and repeat the technique as required.

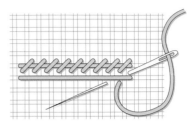

Lay the tramming stitch along the double thread of the canvas and stitch over it.

Choosing stitches

Many canvas-work projects are worked using one basic stitch, with the design shown by changing colors. Small, firm stitches such as tent stitch (p. 178) and half cross-stitch (p. 179) are mostly chosen, and they provide a hard-wearing fabric suitable for upholstery and items that will be subjected to wear.

However, there are many other stitches for canvas, and they can provide an endless range of textures on items such as pictures, where wear is not a consideration. Stitches can be chosen to suit each part of the design, for example circular eyelet stitch (p. 203) for a field of flowers or Scottish squares (p. 220) for a building. Small details such as eyes can be added with a French knot (p. 98) or a small bead (p. 44).

Projects with different stitches are usually worked from line charts (see pp. 19–20). Each stitch is indicated by a different color.

Back stitch

Back stitch (p. 48) is used on canvas work to outline shapes or to cover exposed threads. It can be worked horizontally from right to left, vertically from top to bottom, or diagonally from top right.

In each case work over a regular number of threads or intersections. Bring the needle to the front at A and insert it at B. Bring it out one (or more) holes or intersections beyond.

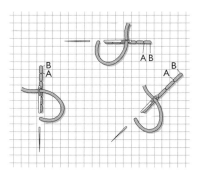

Back stitch worked horizontally, vertically, and diagonally on canvas.

Working in several colors

A variety of effects can be achieved in canvas work by using color, including using two or more colors within the same area.

Stitches worked in rows can be stitched to create stripes. Work each row in turn, fastening off the thread at the end of the row and beginning again with the next color. If the stitch you are using can be worked backward and forward across the area, thread each colored thread on a separate needle. Work the first row, park the needle on the front of the work, work the second row and park that needle, and so on.

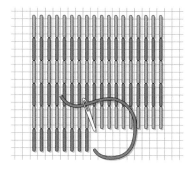

Straight Gobelin stitch (p. 206) worked in two colors.

If stitches are to be worked in alternating colors, work all the stitches in the first color and then go back and fill in the missing stitches with the second color.

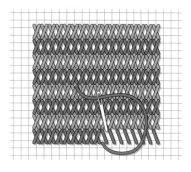

Oblong cross-stitch (p. 192) in two colors.

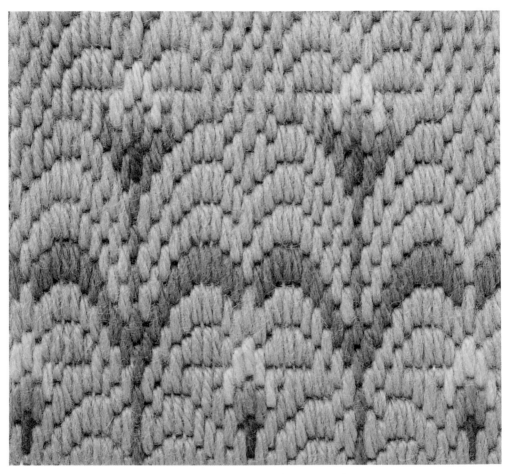

Repeated motifs such as these scallops can be used in Florentine work.

Florentine work

Also known as bargello, Hungarian, or flame work, this technique probably originated in Hungary during the medieval period and spread throughout Europe after it was used in seventeenth-century decorations in the Bargello Palace in Florence. The stitches are vertical and arranged in wavy or zigzag patterns in shaded colors. Stitching is not difficult once the first row establishes the pattern.

Single-mesh canvas and heavy threads will give the best results. The design can be horizontal or in four triangles arranged to make a square. For the latter, chart the triangle carefully so that the four will fit together neatly: Mark the center line and draw the sides at 45-degree angles. Once you have the outline of the triangle, you can plan the design within it. A horizontal design can incorporate small repeating motifs if desired.

Typical stitches
Florentine stitch (p. 211) is often used.

Berlin woolwork
This technique was extremely popular during the nineteenth century. Embroiderers worked with wool threads and followed printed charts that were colored to show the design.

Typical stitches
Tent stitch (p. 178) or cross-stitch (p. 190) were used to create the pictures.

Long stitch
Long stitch is a quick technique for working simple designs and backgrounds. The stitches follow the outlines of the design. If necessary, each area is divided so that stitches are no longer than about ¾ in. (2 cm). Single-mesh canvas and heavy thread will give the best results, with good coverage.

Typical stitches
Long stitch is worked in the same way as straight Gobelin stitch (p. 206), but the length of the stitches varies to fit the design.

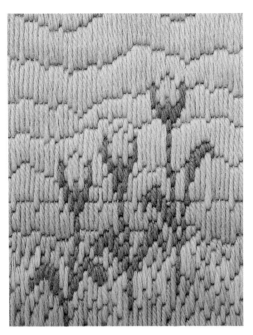

Long stitch lends itself to landscape pictures.

Embroidered rugs
Modern handmade rugs are often worked with wool thread on canvas. For flat rugs, use any hard-wearing stitch, such as the tent stitch (p. 178), diagonal Gobelin stitch (p. 186), cross-stitch (p. 190), and Hungarian stitch (p. 208). Short-pile rugs are often made with Surrey stitch (p. 232).

Both single-mesh and double-mesh canvas are used for making rugs. Rug canvas is usually made from cotton or jute and sometimes contains blue threads at regular intervals.

diagonal stitches

Diagonal canvas stitches are quick and simple to work and include the basic canvas stitches: the tent stitch (petit point) and diagonal Gobelin stitch (gros point). The smaller ones can be used for details, as well as for covering larger areas. Use a tapestry needle.

The diagonal nature of these stitches can distort the canvas, and it will need to be blocked when you have finished the work (see p. 14).

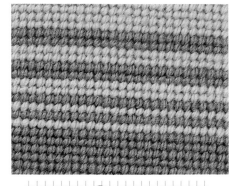

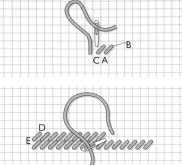

TENT stitch

(Continental stitch, petit point)

This is the smallest and most common canvas stitch. It is worked diagonally over one thread. Work from right to left, beginning with the bottom row, using a tapestry needle.

1. Bring the needle to the front of the canvas at A. Insert the needle at B and then bring it out at C. Continue to the end of the row. The long stitches on the reverse give strength to the work.

2. For the second row, work from the left, stitching each stitch top to bottom (D–E), or turn the canvas and work as before.

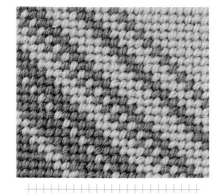

DIAGONAL TENT
stitch

(Basketweave stitch)

This stitch distorts the canvas less than diagonal stitches worked horizontally. Use a tapestry needle and work from top right to bottom left and back up.

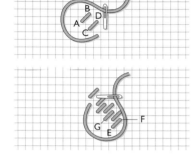

1. Bring the needle to the front of the canvas at A and insert it at B. Then bring it out at C (one hole is left empty), insert it at D, and continue as required.

2. To add a second row, bring the needle out at E and insert it at F, filling the space between the stitches of the previous row. Now take it horizontally across two threads and bring it out at G, as shown. Continue as required.

HALF CROSS-*stitch*

This stitch gives a similar appearance to tent stitch, but the work will look uneven if the two stitches are combined. It uses less thread than tent stitch but is more likely to show wear. The best result is obtained by working on double-mesh canvas. Use a tapestry needle and work from left to right (see upper diagram) or bottom to top (see lower diagram).

1. Bring the needle to the front of the canvas at A.

2. Insert the needle across one intersection at B, and bring it out across one thread at C, as shown at left.

3. Continue to the end of the row.

4. Turn the canvas and work the second row in the same way.

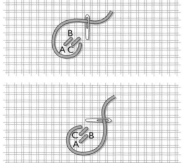

MOSAIC *stitch*

This stitch covers areas with small squares, each consisting of a long stitch between two short ones. Use a tapestry needle.

Working horizontally

1. Bring the needle to the front of the canvas at the top right, at A, and insert it at B. Then bring it out at C.

2. Take the needle up over two intersections and insert it at D. Then bring it out at E, in the same row as B, and insert it over one intersection at F to complete the square, as shown in the upper diagram.

3. Bring the needle out at G, in the hole next to C, and continue to the end of the row, as shown.

4. Turn the canvas around and again work the next row from right to left, as shown in the lower diagram.

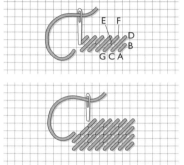

Working diagonally

1. Bring the needle to the front of the canvas at the top left, at A, in the upper diagram.

2. Take the needle up over one intersection and insert it at B. Then bring it out at C, below A, as shown.

3. Take the needle up over two intersections and insert it at D. Then bring it out at E, in the square to the right of C, and insert it over one intersection at F to complete the square, as shown.

4. To begin the next square, bring the needle out at G, two holes below E (one hole is left empty), and continue in the same way, as shown.

5. Work the next row to the right of the first row, starting above the bottom square, as shown in the lower diagram. The long stitch of each square fits into the empty hole, as shown in the lower diagram.

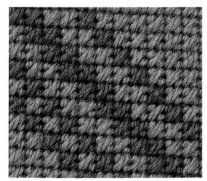

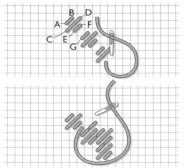

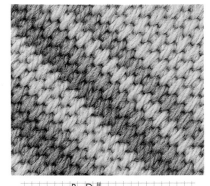

CONDENSED MOSAIC *stitch*

This stitch covers areas with a diagonal interlocked pattern of alternating short and long stitches. Use a tapestry needle and work from the top left to lower right.

1. Bring the needle to the front of the canvas at A. Take it up over one intersection and insert it at B, as shown.

2. Bring it out at C, in the hole below A, and take it up and over two intersections to insert it at D, as shown.

3. Bring it out at E, in the hole to the right of C, and continue to the end of the row, as shown.

4. Work the next row to the right of the first row, starting at the bottom, placing the short stitches against the long ones of the first row and vice versa.

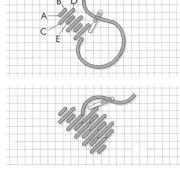

CHECKER *stitch*

Working in one color (horizontally)

Bring a tapestry needle to the front of the canvas at the bottom right, at A, and work a square of Scotch stitch (p. 182). Bring the needle out at B and work a square of nine tent stitches (p. 178), in the order shown in the diagram. Repeat to the end of the row. Turn the canvas and work back, alternating the squares.

Working in two colors (diagonally)

Bring a tapestry needle to the front of the canvas at the top left and work a row of diagonal Scotch stitch (p. 182). Work a second row of diagonal Scotch stitch from bottom to top, so that the corners just touch those of the first row, and continue working rows as required. Begin again at the top left with the second color and work the tent-stitch (p. 178) squares between the rows.

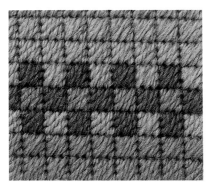

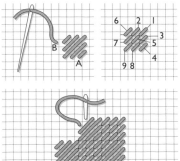

SCOTCH *stitch*

This stitch covers an area with small squares, each consisting of five stitches. Use a tapestry needle.

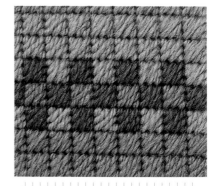

Working horizontally

1. Bring the needle to the front of the canvas at A. Take it up and across one intersection and insert it at B, as shown in the upper diagram.

2. Bring the needle out at C and put it in at D, then out at E and in at F. Bring the needle out at G and insert it at H. To complete the square, bring the needle out at I and insert it at J, as shown.

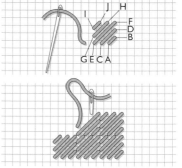

3. Bring the needle out in the hole beside E and continue stitching in the same manner, as shown in the lower diagram, to the end of the row. Turn the canvas and stitch the second row from right to left.

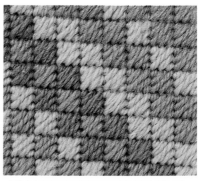

Working diagonally

1. Bring the needle to the front of the canvas at the top left, at A. Take it up and across one intersection and insert it at B, as shown in the upper diagram.

2. Bring the needle out at C and insert it at D, then out at E and in at F. Bring the needle out at G and insert it at H, as shown.

3. To complete the square, bring the needle out at I and insert it at J, as shown.

4. To begin the next block, bring the needle out two holes below J and continue stitching to the end of the row.

5. The second row is worked to the right of the first, from bottom to top, with the longest stitch of each block beginning in the empty hole, as shown in the lower diagram.

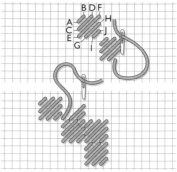

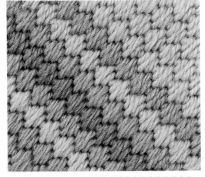

CONDENSED SCOTCH *stitch*

This stitch covers an area with diagonal rows of interlocking blocks, each consisting of four stitches. Use a tapestry needle and work from the top left to lower right.

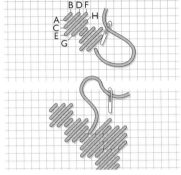

1. Bring the needle to the front of the canvas at the top left, at A and insert it at B, as shown in the upper diagram.

2. Bring the needle out at C and insert it at D, then out at E, in at F, and out at G and in at H, as shown.

3. To begin the next block, bring the needle out in the hole beside G and continue stitching to the end of the row.

4. The second row is worked to the right of the first, from bottom to top, with the smallest stitch beginning against the longest of the first row, as shown in the lower diagram.

MOORISH *stitch*

Working in one color

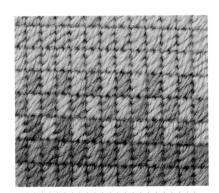

Bring a tapestry needle to the front of the canvas at A and work a row of condensed Scotch stitch (see above). Work a row of diagonal tent stitch (p. 179) to the right and from bottom to top, as shown in the diagram. Continue working alternate rows as required.

Working in two colors

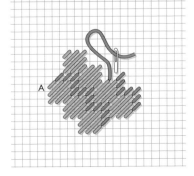

Bring a tapestry needle to the front of the canvas at the top left at A, and work a row of condensed Scotch stitch (see above). Work a second row of condensed Scotch stitch from bottom to top, leaving one intersection bare between the stitches of the two rows. Begin again at the left with the second color and work tent stitch (p. 178) over the bare intersections.

CASHMERE *stitch*

This stitch covers areas with small rectangular blocks, each consisting of two short and two long stitches. Use a tapestry needle.

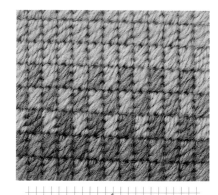

Working horizontally

1. Bring the needle to the front of the canvas at the bottom right at A, and insert it at B. Then bring it out at C and put it in at D, as shown in the upper diagram.

2. Bring it out at E and put it in at F. Now bring it out at G and insert it at H, to complete the block, as shown.

3. To begin the next block, bring the needle out of the hole beside C and continue stitching to the end of the row.

4. Turn the canvas around and work the next row from right to left, as shown in the lower diagram.

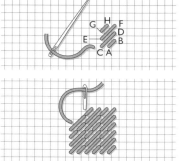

Working diagonally

1. Bring the needle to the front of the canvas at the top left at A, and insert it at B. Then bring it out at C and put it in at D, out at E, and in at F, as shown in the lower-left diagram.

2. Bring it out at G and insert it at H to complete the block.

3. To begin the next block, bring the needle out two holes below H (one hole is left empty) and continue in the same way to the end of the row.

4. The second row is worked to the right of the first, from bottom to top, with the second stitch of each block beginning in the empty hole, as shown in the lower-right diagram.

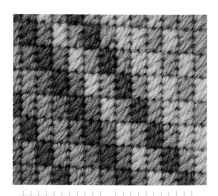

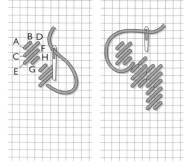

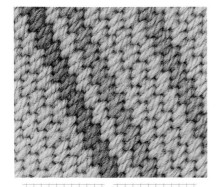

CONDENSED CASHMERE *stitch*

This stitch covers areas with steeply sloping diagonal rows of intersecting rectangles, each consisting of one short stitch and two long ones. Use a tapestry needle.

1. Bring the needle to the front of the canvas at A and insert it at B, as shown in the left diagram.

2. Bring the needle out at C and insert it at D. Then bring it out at E and insert it at F.

3. Now bring it out of the hole to the right of E and continue to the end of the row.

4. The second row is worked to the right of the first row, from bottom to top, as shown in the right diagram.

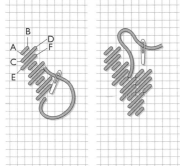

REP *stitch*

This stitch covers areas with gently sloping stitches. When worked over one thread on double-mesh canvas, it is known as Aubusson stitch. Use a tapestry needle and work from the top right to lower left of the area.

1. Bring the needle to the front of the canvas at A.

2. Take the needle up over one horizontal and two vertical threads and insert it at B.

3. Bring it out at C and insert it at D, as shown in left part of the diagram.

4. Continue to the end of the row. Then turn the canvas and work the next row in the same way, as shown in right part of diagram.

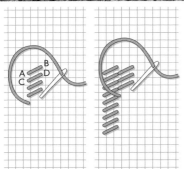

DIAGONAL GOBELIN *stitch*

(Slanted Gobelin stitch, oblique Gobelin stitch, gros point)

This stitch is worked over two to five horizontal threads and one or two vertical ones. Use a tapestry needle and work from the top right.

1. Bring the needle to the front of the canvas at A. Take it up and across the required number of threads and insert it at B. Bring the needle out at C and insert it at D. Continue to the end of the row, as shown in the upper diagram.

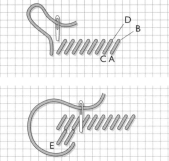

3. For the second row, maintain the same length and slope of the stitches. Bring the needle out at E and insert it into the same hole as the base of the first row, as shown in the lower diagram. Continue working to the right.

ENCROACHING DIAGONAL GOBELIN *stitch*

(Encroaching slanted or oblique Gobelin stitch)

This stitch is usually worked on single-mesh canvas, over two to five horizontal threads and one or two vertical ones. Use a tapestry needle and start working at the top right of the canvas.

1. Bring the needle to the front of the canvas at A and insert it at B. Bring the needle out at C and insert it at D. Continue to the end of the row, as shown in the upper diagram.

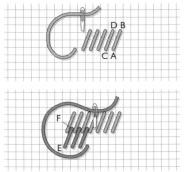

2. For the second row, maintain the same length and slope of the stitches. Bring the needle out at E and insert it into the hole one thread above the base of the first row of stitches, at F. Work additional rows, so that each overlaps the previous one in the same way, as shown.

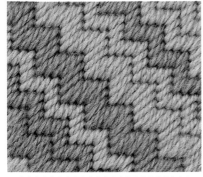

BYZANTINE *stitch*

This stitch covers large areas with broad zigzag bands. Four, six, or eight stitches can be worked in each step, as shown in the photograph at left. Use a tapestry needle and work from the top left to lower right.

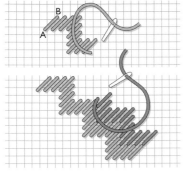

1. Bring the needle to the front of the canvas at A and insert it at B.

2. Bring the needle out of the hole to the right of A and insert it to the right of B, repeating twice to make four stitches, as shown in the upper diagram.

3. Work three stitches below the last stitch. Then work three beside the last one, and continue making equal steps.

4. Work the second row from the bottom to the top, following the steps of the first row, as shown in the lower diagram.

JACQUARD *stitch*

This stitch covers large areas with broad zigzag bands of Byzantine stitch alternating with tent stitches. Four, six, or eight stitches can be worked in each step of the Byzantine work as shown in the photo at left. Use a tapestry needle and work from the top left to bottom right.

1. Bring the needle to the front of the canvas at A and work Byzantine stitch rows (see above) across the area, leaving one intersection bare between the rows, as shown in the diagram.

2. Bring the needle out at bottom right and work tent stitches over the bare intersections, working each stitch from bottom to top (B–C) on the horizontal sections and from top to bottom (D–E) on the vertical ones, as shown.

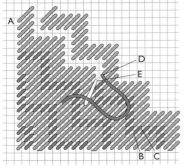

MILANESE *stitch*

This stitch covers areas with a diagonal pattern of interlocking triangles, each triangle consisting of four stitches. Use a tapestry needle and work from the top left to the lower right.

1. Bring the needle to the front of the canvas at A and insert it at B. Bring it out at C and insert it at D. In the same way work stitches from E to F and G to H, as shown in the top diagram.

2. To begin the next triangle, bring the needle out two holes to the right of E. Continue to the end of the row.

3. Begin the second row to the right of the first and work upward from the bottom. Work the triangles in the same way, from smallest stitch to largest, fitting the smallest against the largest of the first row, as shown.

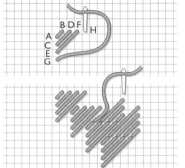

ORIENTAL *stitch*

This stitch covers areas with a diagonal undulating pattern, formed by spaced rows of Milanese stitch and diagonal filling stitches. Use a tapestry needle and work from the top left to lower right.

1. Bring the needle to the front of the canvas at A and work rows of Milanese stitch (see above), spacing the rows so that the longest stitches in each triangle are aligned.

2. Each of the "fillers" consists of three stitches worked over two intersections. Bring the needle out at B and insert it at C. Then bring it out at D and insert it below C, and work the third stitch the same way. Repeat to the end of the row, as shown in the diagram.

3. To fill the second row, bring the needle out at E and work groups of three stitches in the same way.

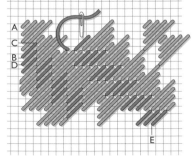

PERSPECTIVE *stitch*

This stitch covers an area with a pattern that can look like interlocked rows of three-dimensional cubes. Use a tapestry needle and work in two shades, from the top left to lower right.

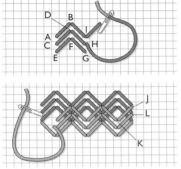

1. Bring the needle to the front of the canvas at A. Take it across two horizontal and two vertical threads and insert it at B, as shown in the upper diagram.

2. Work two parallel stitches from C to D and E to F, and then three opposing stitches, from G to F, H to D, and I to B.

3. Bring the needle out at I and continue to the end of the row in the same manner, ending with a complete pattern. Secure the needle in the margin.

4. Bring the second color to the front at the right-hand end at J. Insert the needle at K and bring it out at L. Continue to make three overlapping stitches and then three opposing ones, always stitching from the outside inward, as shown in the middle diagram.

5. Continue to the end of the row and secure the needle in the margin.

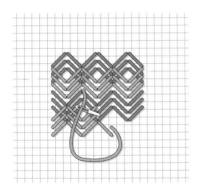

6. Bring the first color to the front at the right-hand end and work a row of stitches parallel to the second row, as shown in the lower diagram. The fourth row overlaps the third row, as before.

crossed
stitches
on canvas

Crossed stitches give a solid, textured effect and good coverage on canvas. Because of the crossing stitches, they tend not to distort the canvas.

For an even result, the stitches on any piece must be worked in the same way so that the upper stitch of each row always lies in the same direction. Use a tapestry needle.

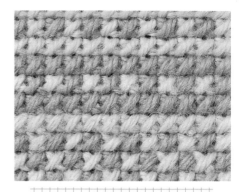

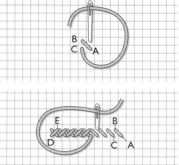

CROSS-*stitch*

This basic canvas stitch, worked on double-mesh canvas, produces a hard-wearing piece. Use a tapestry needle and begin at the top right.

1. Bring the needle to the front of the canvas at A. Take it up and over one intersection and insert it at B.

2. Bring the needle out at C. If working a single cross-stitch, insert it into the hole above A to complete the stitch. If working a row, insert the needle into the hole to the left of B and work to the end of the row.

3. At the end of the row, bring the needle out at D and insert it at E, taking care not to split the thread of the existing stitch. Continue to the end of the row.

UPRIGHT CROSS-
stitch

(St. George's cross-stitch)

This stitch produces an unusual scale pattern. Use a tapestry needle and begin at the top left.

1. Bring the needle to the front of the canvas at A and insert it at B. Bring it out at C and take it over two vertical threads to insert it at D. Bring the needle out two holes to the right of A and continue making crosses to the end of the row, as shown in the upper diagram.

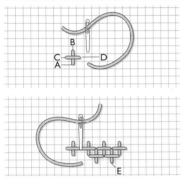

2. To work the second row, bring the needle out at E and work a cross-stitch as in the first row, fitting it against the crosses of the first row, taking care not to split the threads, as shown in the lower diagram.

RICE *stitch*

(Crossed corners cross-stitch)

This stitch can be worked over two or, most often, four threads. Use a tapestry needle and begin at the top right.

Working in one color

Bring the needle to the front of the canvas at A and insert it at B. Bring it out at C and insert it at D to complete the first cross. Make a short stitch over the intersection at each leg, bringing the needle out at E, then F, G, and H. Bring the needle out at C and continue in the same way to the end of the first row.

Working in two colors

Work rows of cross-stitch (see opposite) over the whole area, taking each stitch across two intersections. Bring the second-color thread out at top right and work short stitches over each cross-stitch, in the same order shown at left.

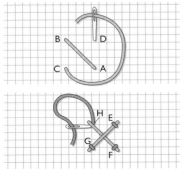

OBLONG CROSS-*stitch*

This stitch is used to cover areas with a pattern of neat horizontal rows of varying height. Use a tapestry needle and begin at the top right.

1. Bring the needle to the front of the canvas at A and insert it at B.

2. Bring the needle out in the hole to the left of A and insert it into the hole to the left of B. Continue to the end of the row.

3. At the end of the row, bring the needle out at C and put it in at D, taking care not to split the thread of the existing stitch above. Continue to the end of the row, working from left to right.

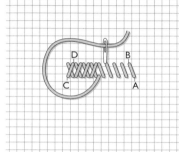

TIED OBLONG CROSS-*stitch*

(Oblong cross-stitch with back stitch)

This stitch is used to cover areas with a pattern of broad horizontal rows of varying height, each incorporating a subtle horizontal line. Use a tapestry needle and begin at the top right.

1. Bring the needle to the front of the canvas at A and insert it at B. Bring it out at C and insert it at D, then out at E and in at F to complete the first stitch, as shown in the top diagram.

2. Bring the needle out in the same hole as C and continue stitching to the end of the row.

3. For the next row, begin at the left. Bring the needle out at G and work an oblong cross-stitch. Then work the tie from right to left (the reverse of the first row). Continue to the end of the row, as shown in the lower diagram.

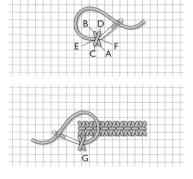

ALTERNATING CROSS-*stitch*

(Double stitch)

This stitch covers an area with a basketweave pattern. Use a tapestry needle and begin at the top left.

1. Bring the needle to the front of the canvas at A and insert it at B. Then bring it out to the left of A and insert it to the right of B to form the oblong stitch, as shown.

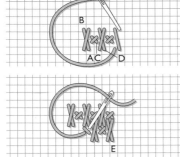

2. Bring the needle out at C and work a cross-stitch over one intersection. Then bring the needle out at D to make the next oblong stitch. Continue to the end of the row.

3. Begin the next row at the right at E, as shown in the lower diagram, and work in the same way, placing oblong stitches under the small stitches and vice versa.

LARGE-AND-SMALL CROSS-*stitch*

(Double cross-stitch)

This stitch covers an area with a pattern of crosses. Use a tapestry needle and begin at the top left.

1. Bring the needle to the front of the canvas at A and insert it at B. Then bring it out at C and insert it at D to complete the large cross. Bring the needle out at E and work an upright cross-stitch over two horizontal and two vertical threads, as shown in the upper diagram.

2. Bring the needle out four holes to the right of A for the next large cross and continue to the end of the row.

3. Bring the needle out at F, as shown in the lower diagram, and work a row of small upright crosses below each large cross. Repeat the first and second rows as required.

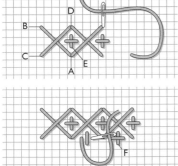

REVERSED CROSS-
stitch

This stitch looks very effective stitched in two shades or colors. Use a tapestry needle and begin at the bottom left.

1. Bring the needle to the front of the canvas at A. Take the needle up across two horizontal and two vertical threads and insert it at B. Bring it out at C and insert it at D to complete the first cross-stitch, as shown in the top diagram.

2. Bring the needle out two holes above D, at E, and make a second cross-stitch. Then bring it out two holes to the right of D, at F, and make another. Make a third stitch diagonally below that to complete the row.

3. Beginning at G, work the next diagonal row of cross-stitches and continue working up and down diagonally across the area.

4. Bring the needle out in the hole above B, at H, as shown in the middle diagram, and work an upright cross over two threads. Continue working rows of upright crosses between the rows of diagonal crosses, making sure the vertical stitch is always on top.

5. Bring the second-color thread out at the bottom left. Work up and down the rows, placing an upright cross over the cross-stitches and vice versa. Make sure that the vertical stitches of the upright crosses are on top and that the diagonal crosses are worked in the same direction as those of the first layer.

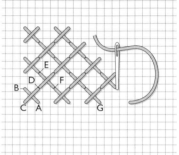

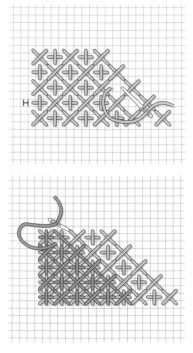

LONG-LEGGED CROSS-*stitch*

(Long-armed cross-stitch, twist stitch, braided Slav stitch)

1. Bring a tapestry needle to the front of the canvas at A and insert it at B. This makes a half stitch (p. 179) to begin the row.

2. Bring the needle out at C and insert it at D, then out at E and in at F, out at G and in at B. Then bring it out at C.

3. Continue, always working into the same two rows of holes and keeping the stitches parallel.

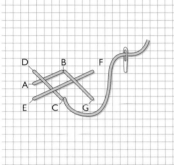

4. To work the second row, either finish off the thread and begin again at the left, or turn the canvas and continue working from left to right to produce a differently textured effect.

MONTENEGRIN CROSS-*stitch*

This stitch also forms a pattern on the back. Use a tapestry needle and begin at the top left.

1. Bring the needle to the front of the canvas at A and insert it at B. This makes a half stitch (p. 179) to begin the row.

2. Bring the needle out at C and insert it at D, then out at E and in at F. Bring it out again at E and insert it at B. Then bring it out yet again at E, as shown.

3. Repeat to the end of the row, always working into the same two rows of holes and keeping the stitches parallel.

4. To work the second row, either finish off the thread and begin again at the left or turn the canvas and continue working to produce a differently textured effect.

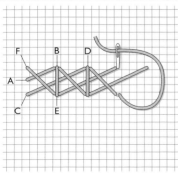

ITALIAN CROSS-
stitch

(Two-sided Italian cross-stitch, arrowhead cross-stitch)

This stitch covers an area with an intricate pattern of boxed crosses. Begin at the top right.

1. Bring a tapestry needle to the front of the fabric at A and insert it across three threads at B. Bring it out at C and insert it again at B, and then bring it out at D and in again at B, as shown in the upper diagram.

2. Bring the needle out again at C and continue making groups of three stitches to the end of the row.

3. Bring the needle out at top left, at E, and insert it at F to make a diagonal stitch. Then bring it out at G and make the next diagonal stitch. Continue along the row.

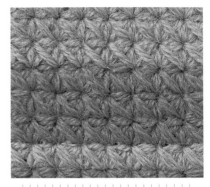

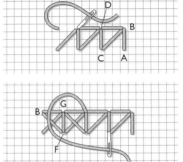

GREEK *stitch*

This stitch covers an area with an irregular pattern of crosses. Use a tapestry needle and begin at the top left.

1. Bring the needle to the front of the canvas at A and insert it across two horizontal and two vertical threads, at B, as shown in the upper diagram.

2. Bring it out at C and insert it at D.

3. Bring the needle out midway between A and D, at E, and insert it two holes to the right of B.

4. Bring it out in the same hole as B and make a second long stitch. Continue to the end of the row and fasten off.

5. Work the second row from the left also, as shown.

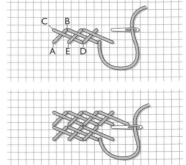

HERRINGBONE
stitch

This stitch is the same as that used on fabric. Worked on canvas, it covers an area with a hard-wearing, tightly woven pattern. It can be worked over two or more threads. Use a tapestry needle and begin at the top left.

1. Bring the needle to the front of the fabric at A.

2. Insert the needle at B and bring it out at C.

3. Then insert it at D and bring it out at E. Continue to the end of the row and fasten off.

4. Work the second row from the left, bringing the needle out one hole below A.

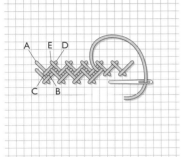

DOUBLE HERRINGBONE *stitch*

This stitch covers an area with a hard-wearing, tightly woven pattern. It uses two colors, with the second making a strong zigzag pattern. Begin at the top left.

1. Bring a tapestry needle to the front of the fabric at A and work one row of herringbone stitch (see above). Fasten off the thread.

2. Bring the needle out two holes below A and work a second row of herringbone from the left. Continue working rows to cover the area, as shown.

3. Bring the second thread to the front at B, two holes below A, and insert it at C. Bring it out at D and insert the needle three holes to the right of B, thus making an upside-down herringbone stitch. Continue to the end of the row and fasten off.

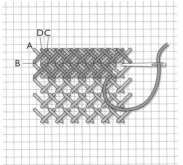

star stitches

Star stitches consist of four or more individual stitches to create a multispoked effect. They include eyelet stitches worked into a center hole, as well as crossing stitches. Most can be used individually for details, or they can be worked over an area to produce a pattern of textured squares or diamonds. Use a tapestry needle.

Within any area, be sure to construct each star in the same order.

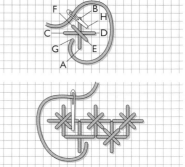

STAR *stitch*

(Double-straight cross-stitch)

Each star consists of a double cross. Work from the top left-hand corner of the area.

1. Bring a tapestry needle to the front at A, insert it at B, then out at C and in at D.

2. Now work a diagonal cross over the upright cross. Bring the needle out at E and insert it at F; then bring it out at G and insert it at H, as shown in the top diagram. Continue stitching to the end of the row.

3. To begin the next star, bring the needle out four holes to the right of A.

4. Begin the next row at the right, placing the stars with their tips touching, as shown.

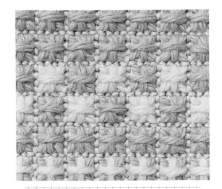

LEVIATHAN *stitch*

(Smyrna stitch)

This stitch covers an area with a pattern of tightly textured squares. Each star consists of a double cross. Work from the top left-hand corner of the area.

1. Bring a tapestry needle to the front at A and insert it at B. Bring it out at C and insert it at D to form a cross.

2. Bring the needle out at E, midway between A and C, and insert it at F, midway between B and D. Then bring it out at G and insert it at H to complete the star.

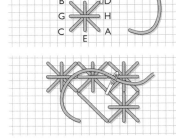

3. Bring the needle out four squares to the right of A to begin the next star and continue to the end of the row. Begin the next row at the right, four holes below the base of the last stitch (see lower diagram).

DOUBLE LEVIATHAN *stitch*

This stitch covers an area with a pattern of raised, textured squares, each consisting of a sixteen-spoked star. Work from the top left-hand corner of the area.

1. Bring a tapestry needle to the front at A and insert it at B. Bring it out at C and insert it at D to form a cross.

2. Bring the needle out at E and insert it at F. Then bring it out at G and insert it at H.

3. Continue working from I to P (see upper diagram).

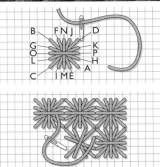

4. Bring the needle out four squares to the right of A to begin the next star and continue to the end of the row.

5. Begin the next row at the right, four holes below the base of the last stitch, and work each star in the same order as before (see lower diagram).

HALF RHODES *stitch*

This stitch covers an area with an interlocked sheaf pattern, each "sheaf" consisting of five stitches. Larger "sheaves" can be made if required. Use a tapestry needle and work from the top right-hand corner of the area.

1. Bring the needle to the front of the canvas at A. Take it over four horizontal and four vertical threads and insert it at B.

2. Bring it out one hole to the right of A, at C, and insert it one hole to the left of B, at D. Then bring it out one hole to the right of C, at E, and insert it one hole to the left of D, at F.

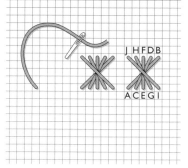

3. Continue working in the same way from G to H and from I to J (see upper diagram).

4. Bring the needle out six holes to the left of A to begin the next group of stitches. There will be one hole left open between the completed groups.

5. Begin the second row in a second color at the left-hand side, bringing the needle out at K, two holes below the last row and two holes to the left of the right-hand edge of the last group of stitches. Work each group of stitches in the same order as in the first row (see lower diagram).

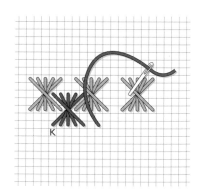

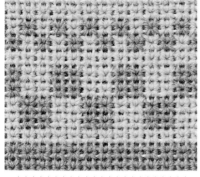

ALGERIAN EYE
stitch
(Star stitch)

This stitch consists of eight spokes, so use single-mesh canvas. Work with a tapestry needle from the top right of the area.

1. Bring the needle to the front of the canvas at A and insert it at the center at B. Bring it out at C and insert it at B. Continue working clockwise, placing one stitch in each hole and finishing by inserting the needle at B.

2. Bring the needle out at H and work the next square in the same order. Continue to the end of the row, as shown.

3. Begin the second row at the left, bringing the needle out at J and working counterclockwise to form each square.

LARGE ALGERIAN EYE *stitch*

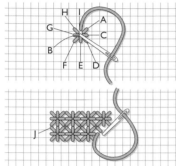

This stitch covers an area with indented squares, twice as large as those of Algerian eye stitch, so it is faster to work. It often shows canvas between the squares, so the back stitch is used around each square. Use a tapestry needle and work from the top right of the area.

1. Bring the needle to the front of the canvas at A.

2. Work Algerian eye stitch (see above), but stitch over two threads or intersections instead of one.

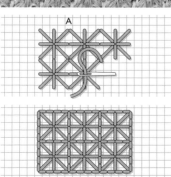

3. Bring the needle out at the top right and work back stitches (see p. 175) between each square.

DIAMOND EYELET
stitch

This stitch covers an area with a pattern of diagonally arranged diamonds. Each one consists of sixteen spokes made into a center hole, so single-mesh canvas and fine thread will give the best results. The four main spokes are longer, to create the diamond shape. Use a tapestry needle and work from the top-left corner of the area.

1. Bring the needle to the front of the canvas at A. Take it over four threads and insert it at the center at B.

2. Bring it out in the hole below and to the right of A, at C, and insert it at B. Continue working clockwise around the diamond, placing one stitch in each hole and finishing by inserting the needle at B for each stitch, as shown in the top diagram. If preferred, the stitch may be worked counterclockwise.

3. Bring the needle out eight holes to the right of A and work the next diamond in the same order. Continue to the end of the row.

4. Begin the next row at the right end, fitting each diamond between the lower parts of those of the first row and working into the same holes, as shown in the middle diagram. The diamonds may be worked clockwise or counterclockwise, but work the whole row the same way.

5. Continue as required, repeating these two rows.

6 If the coverage of the canvas is incomplete, work back stitch (see p. 175) between each diamond, as shown in the bottom diagram.

CIRCULAR EYELET
stitch
(Daisy stitch)

This stitch covers an area with a pattern of circular eyelets. Each one consists of sixteen spokes made into a center hole, so single-mesh canvas and fine thread will give the best results. All spokes are the same length. Work from the top right-hand corner of the area.

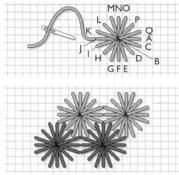

1. Bring a tapestry needle to the front of the canvas at A. Take it over three threads and insert it at the cente, at B, shown in the upper diagram.

2. Bring the needle out at C and insert it at B. Continue working clockwise around the circle, placing one stitch in each hole and finishing by inserting the needle at B, as shown.

3. Bring the needle out again at J and work the next circle in the same order, placing the spokes C and Q in the same holes as I and K of the first circle, as shown in the lower diagram. Continue to the end of the row.

4. Begin the next row at the left end, fitting each circle between the lower parts of those of the first row and working into the same holes. Continue as required, repeating these two rows, as shown in the lower diagram.

Large and small circles

These are usually worked in two shades for added contrast. Work rows of circular eyelet stitches, aligning the rows and placing the top three stitches of each circle in the same holes as the bottom three of the circles in the previous row. Start again at the top right with a second-color thread and stitch rows of twelve-spoked circles in the gaps, as shown at left. Work these small circles in the same order as the larger ones.

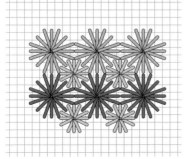

WINDMILL *stitch*

(Pinwheel stitch)

This stitch forms a pattern of irregular motifs that resemble
the sails on a windmill. They can be stitched in rows or
scattered randomly. The background is filled with diagonal
stitches (tent stitch or longer). Eight stitches are made into a
center hole, so single-mesh canvas will give the best results.
Begin each motif at the right. Use a tapestry needle and
mark the top of the canvas before you start.

1. Bring the needle to the front of the canvas at A and take it
over seven vertical threads and insert it at B. Bring it out at C
and take it over five threads to insert it at D, as shown at right.

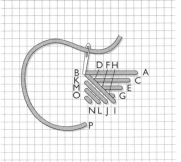

2. Bring the needle out at E and take it over three
threads and insert it at F. Then bring it out at G and take
it over one thread to insert it at H, as shown at right.

3. Bring the needle out at I and insert it at B. Bring it out at
J and insert it at K. Repeat twice from L to M and N to O.
Bring the needle out at P, as shown in the upper diagram.

4. Turn the canvas 90 degrees to the right. Cross seven
threads and insert the needle at B. Repeat steps 1 to 3.
Do this twice more to complete the motif, as shown in
the middle diagram.

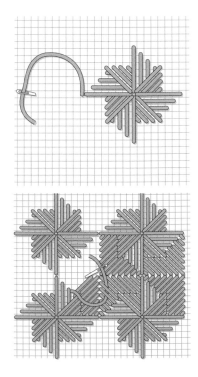

5. Turn the canvas right way up and bring the needle out at
the end of the left stitch. Stitch more motifs as required.

6. Begin the next row at the left, working the long arms
into the same holes as those of the first row.

7. Fill the blank areas between motifs. If using long diagonal
stitches, as shown at right, bring the needle out around the
motif for each stitch, turning the canvas when stitching the
motif.

PETAL *stitch*

This stitch covers an area with a pattern of rayed crosses over circles of thread. They can be stitched in rows or scattered randomly, with the background filled with contrasting stitches. Make twenty stitches into a center hole (B), and use single-mesh canvas and a fine thread for the rays for best results. This is a decorative stitch, but it is not hard-wearing. Use a tapestry needle and begin each motif at the top right-hand corner.

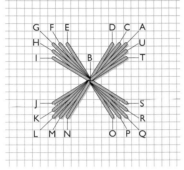

1. Bring the needle to the front of the canvas at A.

2. Take the needle over five vertical and five horizontal threads and insert it at B at the center. Bring it out at C and insert it at B. Then bring it out at D and insert it at B.

3. Leave five holes blank and bring the needle out at E. Continue working counterclockwise around the square until there are five rays in each group, as shown in the top diagram.

4. To begin the next motif, bring the needle out of the same hole as G or A. Rows may be worked in either direction. Stitch as many rows as required.

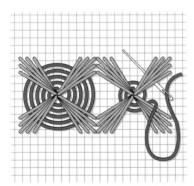

5. Bring the thread for the circles to the front of the canvas in the hole above B, as shown in the middle diagram. Working counterclockwise, slide the needle through under the four groups of rays and above the canvas. Keep working in a spiral, keeping the turns closely packed and arranging them so they lie flat. Insert the needle under one group of rays.

6. Work four straight stitches at each corner between motifs to completely cover the canvas, as shown in the lower diagram.

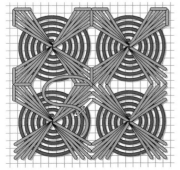

straight stitches

Straight stitches are worked parallel with the canvas threads. To cover the canvas completely, you will usually need to use a thick thread and a tapestry needle. The stitches are quick and easy to work and are ideal for covering large areas.

Straight stitches can be used to achieve a variety of shading effects when worked in more than one color.

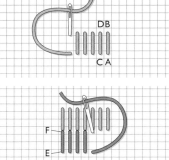

STRAIGHT GOBELIN *stitch*

(Upright Gobelin stitch)

This stitch is worked over two or more threads. Use a tapestry needle and start at the top right.

1. Bring the needle to the front at A and insert it over the required number of threads at B (see upper diagram).

2. Bring it out at C and insert it at D. Continue to the end of the row.

3. Bring the needle out at E and insert it at F, in the same hole as the bottom of the last stitch of the previous row. The stitch should be over three threads, as in the previous row (see lower diagram).

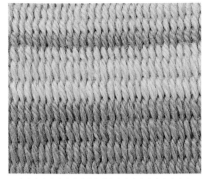

ENCROACHING STRAIGHT GOBELIN *stitch*

(Encroaching upright Gobelin stitch)

This stitch is worked over two or more threads. Use a tapestry needle and work from top right to bottom left.

1. Bring the needle to the front of the canvas at A and insert it over the required number of threads at B. Bring it out at C and insert it at D. Work to the end of the row.

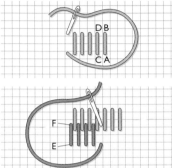

2. Bring the needle out at E and insert it at F, so that the stitch formed is to the left of the last stitch in the previous row and overlaps it. Continue stitching to the end of the row, always inserting the needle to the left of the stitch above.

GOBELIN FILLING *stitch*

(Large brick stitch)

This stitch is worked over any even number of threads. Work from top right to bottom left.

1. Bring the needle to the front of the canvas at A and insert it over the required number of threads at B. Bring it out at C, leaving an empty hole between A and C, and insert it at D. Continue to the end of the row (see upper diagram).

2. Begin the next row by bringing the needle out at E and inserting it at F, so that the stitch overlaps the last row by two threads and lies between the stitches in the row above. Continue to the end of the row.

3. Begin the third row at the right and place each stitch so that the top is in the same hole as the base of a stitch in the first row (see lower diagram)

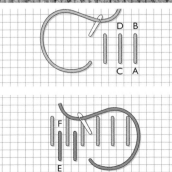

HUNGARIAN *stitch*

This stitch creates a pattern of diagonally arranged diamonds. Work from top right to bottom left.

1. Bring a tapestry needle to the front of the canvas at A and insert it at B. Bring it out at C and insert it at D. Then bring it out at E and insert it at F to complete the unit (see upper diagram).

2. Bring the needle out two holes to the left of E, leaving one hole blank, and continue to the end of the row.

3. Begin the second row at the left and work backward, staggering the units so that the center stitch fits into the blank hole (see lower diagram).

4. Begin the third row at the right, placing the units so the long stitch is below the long stitch of the first row.

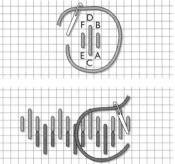

HUNGARIAN DIAMOND *stitch*

This stitch creates a pattern of diagonally arranged larger diamonds. Work from top right to bottom left.

1. Bring the needle to the front of the canvas at A and put it in over two threads at B. Bring it out at C and insert it over four threads at D. Then bring it out at E and insert it over six threads at F (see upper diagram).

2. Now bring it out at G and insert it over four threads at H. Then bring it out at I and insert it over two threads at J to complete the unit. Leave one hole blank and stitch another unit to the left, continuing as required.

3. Begin the second row at the left, staggering the units so that the center stitch fits into the blank hole. Begin the third row at the right, working so the long stitch is below the long stitch of the first row (see lower diagram).

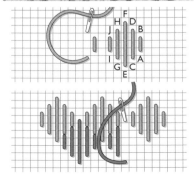

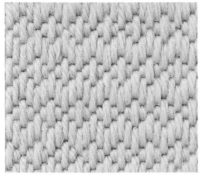

HUNGARIAN GROUNDING

This stitch creates a pattern of rows of small diamonds with zigzag rows between. It can be worked in two colors. Start each row at the right if working in two colors. (The diamonds can be worked from left to right if using only one color.) Use a tapestry needle.

1. Bring the needle to the front of the canvas at A. Take it up and over four threads and insert it at B (see upper diagram).

2. Bring the needle out at C and put it in over four threads at D. Repeat from E to F.

3. Bring the needle out at G and insert it at H. Repeat from I to J. Continue working two stitches upward and two downward to the end of the row.

4. Begin the second row at the right, bringing the needle out at K, two holes below C, and inserting it into the same hole as C. Then bring it out four holes below E, at L, and insert it at E. Bring it out two holes below G, at M, and insert it at G to complete one diamond (see middle diagram).

5. Leave one hole blank and continue to the end of the row.

6. Repeat the first and second rows (see bottom diagram).

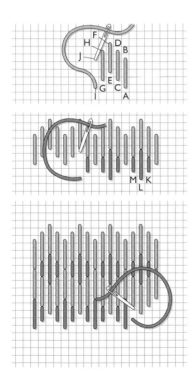

PARISIAN *stitch*

This stitch creates a dense basketweave pattern that is easy to stitch. Work from top right to bottom left.

1. Bring a tapestry needle to the front of the canvas at A. Take it up and over two threads and insert it at B.

2. Bring it out at C and take it up and over four threads and insert it at D (see upper diagram).

3. Continue working short and long stitches to the end of the row.

4. Begin at the left and work the next row in the same way, placing the short stitches under the long ones of the previous row and the long stitches under the short ones (see lower diagram).

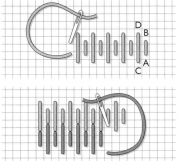

OLD FLORENTINE *stitch*

This stitch creates a large basketweave pattern that is easy to stitch. The short stitches can be worked over any number of threads, with the long ones always worked over three times that number. Work from top right to bottom left.

1. Bring the needle to the front of the canvas at A. Take it up and over two threads and insert it at B. Work a second stitch in the same way, from C to D (see upper diagram).

2. Bring it out at E and take it up and over six threads to insert it at F. Work a second stitch in the same way, from G to H. Repeat these four stitches to the end of the row.

3. Begin at the left and work the next row in the same way, placing the short stitches under the long ones of the previous row and the long stitches under the short ones (see lower diagram).

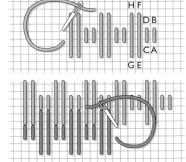

FLORENTINE *stitch*

(Flame stitch, bargello stitch, cushion stitch, Irish stitch)

This stitch produces a zigzag or flame pattern and can be worked in one or more colors. The stitch can be worked over any number of threads; the steps can also be any size, as long as they are shorter than the stitches. All stitches in a row should be the same length, but the length can vary from row to row if desired. The zigzags can be regular (see top photograph) or curving for a flamelike effect (see lower photograph). To produce the curving shape, vary the steps between stitches; the length of the stitches should always be the same. Start work at the top, in the center of the first row, to ensure a regular pattern.

1. Bring a tapestry needle to the front of the canvas at A. Take it up and insert it at B, over four threads (see upper diagram).

2. Bring the needle out at C and take it up and over four threads and insert it at D. Repeat twice, from E to F and from G to H.

3. Then bring the needle out to the left and two holes above G and work three stitches going up.

4. Continue working three stitches down and up to the left end of the row, and work from the center to the right end of the row in the same way.

5. Begin the next row at left or right and work to the end of the row (see lower diagram), continuing rows as required.

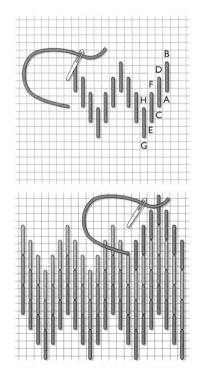

DARNING *stitch*

This stitch creates a pattern of regular vertical rows with ribs between. Work from top right to bottom left.

1. Bring a tapestry needle to the front of the canvas at A. Insert it at B, bring it out at C, and insert it at D, making each stitch the same length and the stitches longer than the spaces between them (see upper diagram).

2. Continue to the end of the row.

3. Turn the canvas around and bring the needle out at E, below the existing stitch. Take care not to catch the thread. Insert the needle in at F, below the existing stitch, and continue to the end of the row (see lower diagram).

4. Turn the canvas and continue stitching rows as required.

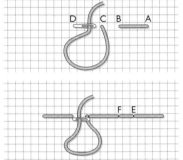

BRICK *stitch*

This stitch creates a dense, overall pattern that is easy to stitch. Work from top right to bottom left.

1. Bring a tapestry needle to the front of the canvas at A. Take it up and over two threads and insert it at B.

2. Bring it out at C and take it up and over two threads and insert it at D (see upper diagram).

3. Bring it out at E and take it up and over two threads to insert it at F. Continue to the end of the row.

4. Begin at the left and work the first stitch of the second row from G to H over two threads. Continue to the end of the row, placing a stitch below each stitch of the previous row and taking each stitch over two threads (see lower diagram).

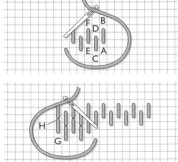

LONG-STITCH TRIANGLES

This stitch is used for covering large areas or borders. It consists of triangles of an even number of stitches (four to eight) arranged to form zigzags (see top photo) or a diamond pattern (see lower photo). Use a tapestry needle and begin at the top right.

1. Bring the needle to the front of the canvas at A and insert it over one thread at B (see first diagram).

2. Bring the needle out at C and insert it over two threads at D. Then bring it out at E and insert it over three threads at F.

3. For a four-stitch triangle, now make a shorter stitch to complete the unit. For a six-stitch triangle, make one more longer stitch, from G to H (see first diagram) and then two shorter stitches, from I to J and K to L. For an eight-stitch triangle, make two longer stitches and then three shorter ones.

4. Continue stitching triangles to the end of the row.

5. For the next row, bring the needle out at M and stitch triangles in reverse to complete one band (see second diagram).

6. Repeat these two rows as required to make more bands. To create a zigzag pattern repeat the first band (see third diagram). For a diamond pattern, stitch the second band as a mirror image of the first (see fourth diagram).

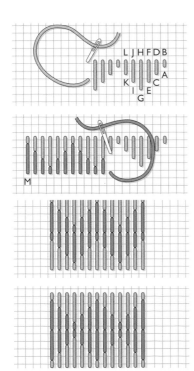

fan stitches

Fan stitches consist of units in which the individual stitches are worked diagonally so that they fan out to create shell-like or leaflike patterns. They produce a textured filling for larger areas.

The stitches that fan out from a single point will give the best results when they are worked on single-mesh canvas, since a number of stitches have to pass through one hole. For the same reason, always use fine thread and a tapestry needle.

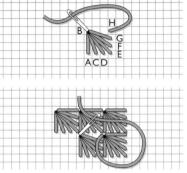

RAY *stitch*

(Fan stitch)

For the best results, use single-mesh canvas, as seven stitches go into one hole. Begin at the top left of the area.

1. Bring a tapestry needle to the front at A and insert it at B. Work stitches from the three holes to the right of A—from C to B, D to B, and E to B. Then work three more from the three holes above E—from F to B, G to B, and H to B—to complete the fan.

2. Bring the needle out at E and work the next fan in the same way. Continue to the end of the row, as shown. Begin the second row at the right, working each fan as before.

EXPANDED RAY *stitch*

(Fxpanded fan stitch)

For the best results, use single-mesh canvas, as thirteen stitches go into one hole. Use a tapestry needle and begin at the top left of the area to be covered.

1. Bring the needle to the front at A and insert it at B. Work stitches from the three holes below A—from C to B, D to B, and E to B. Then work six stitches from the holes to the right of E, all into B—from F, G, H, I, J, and K. Then work stitches from the three holes above K—L, M, and N—into B to complete the fan (see upper diagram).

2. Bring the needle out at N for the next fan. Begin the second row at the right below, and work each fan in reverse.

FANTAIL *stitch*

This stitch creates a pattern of fan-shaped units, each worked from a single hole. The gaps between are filled with a small "tailed" fan. For the best results, use single-mesh canvas, as sixteen stitches go into one hole. Begin at the top left of the area to be covered.

1. Bring the needle to the front at A and insert it at B. Bring the needle out at C and insert it at B, then out at D and in at B, continuing around the fan until fifteen stitches are completed (see upper diagram).

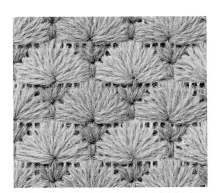

2. Bring the needle out one hole from P and work the next fan in the same way. Continue to the end of the row. Begin the second row at the right and work each fan in reverse.

3. Fill the gaps between the fans with small fans and "tails" (see lower diagram).

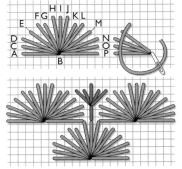

LEAF *stitch*

This stitch creates an overall pattern of leaf-shaped units. Begin at the top left of the area to be covered.

1. Bring a tapestry needle to the front of the canvas at A. Insert the needle at B (see upper diagram).

2. Bring the needle out at C and insert it at D. In the same way make a stitch from E to F.

3. Bring the needle out at G and insert it at H. In the same way make stitches from I to J and K to L. (The last will be vertical.)

4. Bring the needle out at I and work down the opposite side in reverse to complete the leaf.

5. Bring the needle out six holes to the right of A and work the next leaf. Continue to the end of the row.

6. To work the second row, bring the needle out six holes below and three holes to the left of the base of the last leaf (see lower diagram). Work each leaf in reverse.

Back stitch spine

If desired, a row of back stitch can be worked up the center of each leaf (see lower photograph). Begin at the base of the leaf and work six back stitches (see p. 175) on each. If the back stitches are to be in the same color as the leaves, they can be added as each leaf is completed. Otherwise they can be worked once all leaves have been stitched.

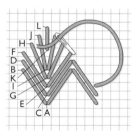

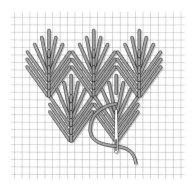

DIAGONAL LEAF *stitch*

This stitch produces a pattern of neat diagonal leaf shapes.

1. Bring a tapestry needle to the front seven holes in from the top-right edge of the area to be covered, at A, and insert it at B. Bring it out at C and insert it at B. Then bring it out at D and insert it at E. Repeat from F to G. Now bring it out at H and insert it at I. Repeat from J to K.

2. Work up the opposite side in reverse to complete the leaf (see upper diagram). To begin the next leaf, bring the needle out three holes to the left of F. Continue as required.

3. Begin the second row from the bottom, working each leaf in the same order as before and fitting them into the first row (see lower diagram).

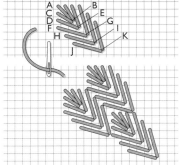

SHELL *stitch*

(Fan stitch, scallop stitch)

This stitch creates shell-shaped units, each worked from a single hole. For the best results, use single-mesh canvas and a tapestry needle. Begin at the bottom right of the area to be covered.

1. Bring the needle to the front at A and insert it at B. Bring it out at C and insert it at B, continuing in the same way (see upper diagram) until you have seven stitches. Bring the needle out at I, one hole below B, and insert it at B to complete the shell.

2. Bring the needle out again at H and work the next shell. Continue to the end of the row (see lower diagram).

3. Begin the second row at the left, bringing the needle out at B. Work the seven long stitches in reverse order.

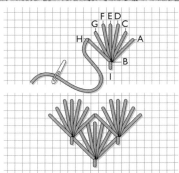

square
stitches

Square stitches cover an area
with a pattern of small square
motifs. The size of the motifs
can be varied from piece to
piece and within a piece. These
stitches give good coverage and
are useful when working
geometric designs and for
details such as brickwork. For
the best results, use a tapestry
needle.

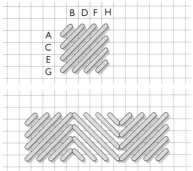

CUSHION *stitch*

(Diagonal satin blocks)

These squares can be any size, and the
stitches can slope from left to right or
from right to left. Squares with opposite
slopes can be combined to form larger
patterns (see photograph). Begin at the
top left of the area to be covered.

1. Bring a tapestry needle to the front at
A. Insert it at B. Bring it out at C, in at D,
out at E, in at F, and then out at G and in
at H (see upper diagram).

2. Continue to form a square of the
required size, always working the stitches
in the same direction (see lower diagram).

CROSSED CUSHION
stitch

This stitch creates an overall pattern of square units. It is worked on a base of cushion stitch (see photograph) and either a single crossing stitch is added (see top diagram) or half the base square can be covered with crossing stitches (see lower diagram). The squares can be any size and the stitches can slope from left to right or from right to left. Squares can be combined to form various patterns. Begin at the top left of the area to be covered.

1. Bring a tapestry needle to the front of the canvas at A. Insert it at B.

2. Bring the needle out at C and insert it at D; then bring it out at E and insert it at F.

3. Continue to form a square of the required size, always working the stitches in the same direction (see diagram 1).

4. Complete all the required cushion-stitch squares.

5. Bring the needle out at G and insert it at H to make a crossing stitch (see diagram 2).

6. If required, bring the needle out at I and insert it at J, continuing to cover half the base square with crossing stitches (see diagram 3 and 4).

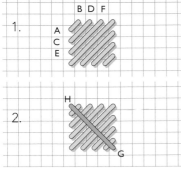

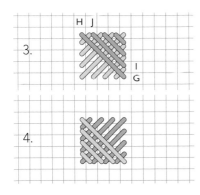

SQUARE EYELET

Each eyelet has sixteen spokes into a center hole, so single-mesh canvas and fine thread will give the best results. The four corner spokes are longer to create the square shape. Construct each square in the same order. Work from the top-left corner of the area.

1. Bring a tapestry needle to the front of the canvas at A and insert it at the center at B. Add stitches from C, D, E, and F to B. Continue working counterclockwise around the square, placing one stitch in each hole, and finish by inserting the needle at B.

2. Bring the needle out at F and work the next square in the same order. Continue to the end of the row. Begin the next row at the top-left corner and again work each square counterclockwise.

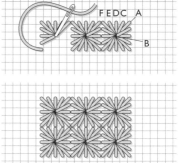

SCOTTISH *squares*

(Scottish stitch)

The overall grid of this stitch may be any size and is often worked in a different color from the filling squares. Start at the top-right corner of the area.

1. Bring the needle to the front of the canvas at A with thread for the grid. Work the horizontal grid lines, using the tent stitch (p. 178) over one or two canvas threads, as desired. Using tent stitch, work the vertical grid lines.

2. For the filling squares, bring the needle out at B and insert it over one intersection at C, slanting it in the same direction as the tent stitch. Bring the needle out at D and insert it at E. Continue until the square is filled. Repeat for each square area (see lower diagram).

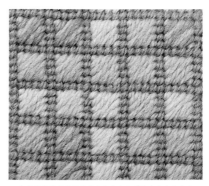

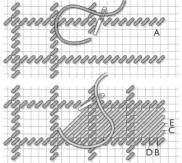

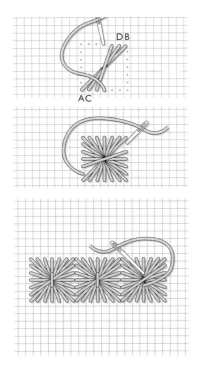

RHODES *stitch*

This stitch creates a pattern of highly textured squares. The squares may be any size and can be worked clockwise or counterclockwise. If they are large, it is useful to add a tying stitch to keep the last stitch in place (see lower photograph). Work from the top left-hand corner of the area.

1. Bring a tapestry needle to the front of the canvas at A, at the lower left-hand corner of the square, and insert it at B, at the top right-hand corner.

2. Bring it out at C and insert it at D, so that it crosses over the first stitch.

3. Continue working around the square, moving one hole each way for each stitch (see upper two diagrams).

4. If required, make a small tie stitch over the last stitch to hold it in place, positioning it as close to the center of the square as possible (see lowest diagram).

5. Bring the needle out at the lower right-hand corner of the first square and work the next square. Continue to the end of the row (see lowest diagram).

HELPFUL HINT

If the canvas is visible between squares, it can be covered by working back stitch (p.175) along each horizontal line and then each vertical one. The same color thread can be used or try a contrasting one for a different effect.

NORWICH *stitch*

(Waffle stitch)

This stitch creates a pattern of squares with a woven effect. The squares may be any size, but are best worked over an uneven number of threads (see top photograph). If worked over an even number (see lower photograph), the center hole on each side of the square is left empty. Start at the top-left corner of the area.

1. Bring a tapestry needle to the front of the canvas at the lower-left corner of the square, at A, and insert it at the top-right corner at B (see upper diagram).

2. Then bring it out at the top-left corner, at C, and insert it at the bottom-right corner at D.

3. Bring the needle out one hole above A, at E, and insert it at F to make a stitch parallel to A–B. Then bring it out one hole to the right of C, at G, and insert it at H to make a stitch parallel to C–D.

4. Continue working stitches (see upper diagram) until all holes have been used (see lower diagram). (The number of stitches required will depend on the size of your square.)

5. If desired, the last stitch can be taken under a previous one at one end (in the lower diagram AA–BB is taken under U–V) to complete the symmetrical arrangement of threads.

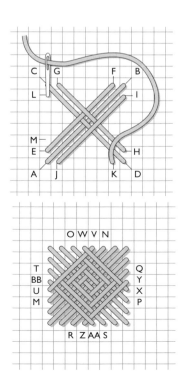

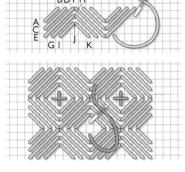

BRIGHTON *stitch*

In this stitch, upright cross-stitches (p. 190) fill the gaps between the tessellated units of diagonal stitches. Use a tapestry needle and start at the top-left corner of the area.

1. Bring the needle to the front of the canvas at A and insert it at B. Bring it out at C and insert it at D. Continue stitching from E to F, G to H, and I to J (see upper diagram).

2. Bring the needle out at K and work five stitches in the opposite direction. Continue to the end of the row.

3. Turn the canvas and stitch the second row, making sure that each unit slopes in the opposite way from the one above it.

4. Stitch an upright cross-stitch (see p. 191) in each gap between units (see lower diagram).

TRIANGLE SQUARES

(Triangle stitch)

This stitch creates a pattern of triangles grouped into squares. Cross-stitches at the corners form small squares. Start at the top-right corner of the area.

1. Bring a tapestry needle to the front of the canvas at A and insert it at B. Now bring the needle out at C and insert it at D. Repeat for stitches from E to F and G to H. Bring the needle out at I and insert it at J. Repeat for stitches from K to L and M to N (see upper diagram).

2. Turn the canvas 90 degrees clockwise, bring the needle out at M, and work another triangle. Repeat twice to complete the square. Work other squares as required.

3. At the corners of the squares, work a cross-stitch.

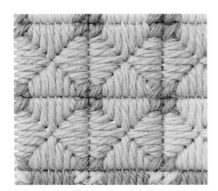

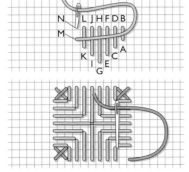

EASTERN *stitch*

This stitch creates a pattern of squares with an open, lacy effect. The canvas is not completely covered, but single-mesh canvas and smooth silk or cotton will look best. For added decorative effect, Eastern stitch can be worked over other stitches, such as Scotch stitch (p. 182) (see lower photograph). Use a tapestry needle and work from the bottom left-hand corner of the area.

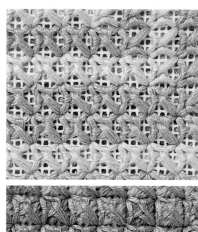

1. Bring the needle to the front of the canvas at A. Take it over four threads and insert it at B.

2. Bring the needle out at C and insert it at A.

3. Bring the needle out at D, loop it around, and slide it along on top of the canvas, under C–A from the left to the right. Keep the needle above the working thread (see upper diagram).

4. Again loop the thread up and slide the needle under A–B from the top downward. Keep the needle above the threads, as shown.

5. Insert the needle at D and bring it out at B.

6. Work the next square as before and continue to the end of the row (see middle diagram).

7. Begin the second row at the right, but work each square in the same order as before.

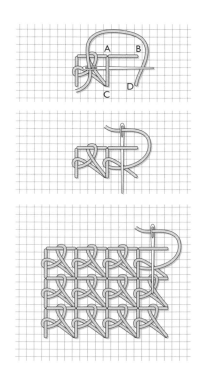

braid and knot stitches

Stitches that create a braided effect can be used to cover large areas of canvas with a dense, intricate pattern of parallel bands. They give good canvas coverage and are often best worked on double-mesh canvas with a tapestry needle.

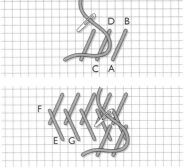

BRAID *stitch*

This stitch covers an area with a pattern of braided horizontal bands. Use a tapestry needle and start at the top-right corner.

1. Bring the needle to the front of the canvas at A and insert it at B. Bring the needle out at C and make a similar stitch to D. Repeat to the end of the row.

2. To begin the second row, bring the needle out at E. Insert it at F. Bring it out at G and continue to the end of the row.

3. Work the third row in the same way. After the first row, the top of the second row will be worked into the same holes as the base of the first row.

ALGERIAN BRAID
stitch

(Knotted stitch)

This stitch covers an area with a pattern of small, tightly braided, horizontal bands. Double-mesh canvas gives the best results. Start at the lower-left corner of the area.

1. Bring a tapestry needle to the front of the canvas at A and insert it at B.

2. Bring the needle out at C and insert it at D. Then bring it out at E and continue to the end of the row (see upper diagram).

3. Begin the second row at the left again, continuing as required (see lower diagram).

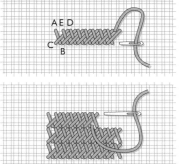

BRAIDED GOBELIN *stitch*

This stitch creates interlocked braided, horizontal bands. Double-mesh canvas gives the best results. Start at the top- or bottom-right corner of the area.

1. Bring a tapestry needle to the front of the canvas at A and insert it at B.

2. Bring the needle out at C and continue making parallel stitches to the end of the row (see upper diagram).

3. To begin the second row, bring the needle out at D, one hole below and one to the left of the base of the last stitch, and insert it at E, one hole above the base of the last stitch in the first row. Continue to the end of the row.

4. Work additional rows as required, each one overlapping the previous row (see lower diagram).

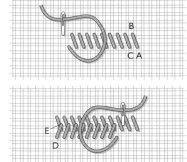

TIED GOBELIN
stitch
(Knotted stitch)

This stitch covers an area with a dense pattern of knotted stitches. Rows overlap, so this stitch is useful for shading. Use a tapestry needle and work from the top right.

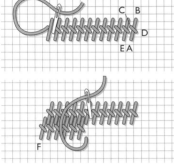

1. Bring the needle to the front of the canvas at A and insert it at B. Bring it out at C and insert it at D to tie the long stitch. Now bring the needle out at E and continue to the end of the row (see upper diagram).

2. To begin the second row, bring the needle out at F and insert it into the same hole as the base of the last tied stitch, (see lower diagram). Continue to the end of the row, slanting the long stitches and the tied stitches in the same direction as the first row.

FRENCH *stitch*

This stitch covers an area with a dense pattern of knotted stitches. The tied stitches form strong horizontal lines through the area. Use a tapestry needle and start at the top right of the area.

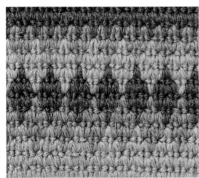

1. Bring the needle to the front of the canvas at A and insert it over four threads, at B. Bring it out at C with the thread to the left of stitch A–B and insert it at D, across one thread to the right, to pull the stitch to the side.

2. Make another stitch from A to B. Bring it out at C with the thread to the right of stitch A–B and then from C to E to complete the first diamond. Bring the needle out at F to begin the next shape. Continue to the end of the row.

3. To begin the next row, bring the needle out at G and insert it at H. Then bring it out at I and insert it at J. Continue to the end of the row.

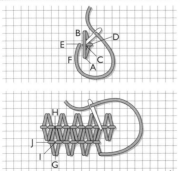

ROCOCO *stitch*

(Queen stitch)

1. Bring a tapestry needle to the front of the canvas, at A, and insert it over four threads at B.

2. Bring it out at C, keeping the thread of A–B on the right, and insert it at D, across one thread, to pull the stitch to the side and make a tie (see upper diagram).

3. Make a second stitch from A to B and a tie from E to C. Make a third stitch from A to B and a tie from F to E, and then a fourth stitch A to B and a tie from G to F.

4. Bring the needle out at H to begin the next shape. To begin the next row, bring the needle out at I and work a shape from left to right. Continue to the end of the row.

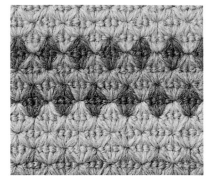

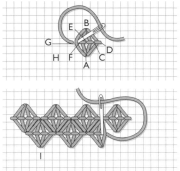

STEM *stitch*

This stitch covers an area with a pattern of strongly ridged, vertical bands. The stitches may be worked over more intersections if desired. Start working from the top.

1. Bring a tapestry needle to the front of the canvas at A and insert it over two intersections to the left at B (see left part of diagram).

2. Bring the needle out at C and insert it at D. Continue to the bottom of the area.

3. To work the return row, bring the needle out at E and put it in over two intersections to the right, at F. Continue to the top of the row (see right diagram).

4. Bring the needle out in the hole above A and put it into A. Then bring it out at C and insert it at A. Continue working back stitches down the spine (see p. 175).

FERN *stitch*

This stitch covers an area with a pattern of neat vertical bands. Use a tapestry needle and start at the top left of the area.

1. Bring the needle to the front of the canvas at A and insert it two holes down and two to the right, at B.

2. Bring it out at C and insert it at D.

3. Bring the needle out in the hole below A and continue making stitches to the bottom of the area (see left part of diagram).

4. To work a second row begin again at the top, bringing the needle out at D (see right part of diagram). Continue as desired.

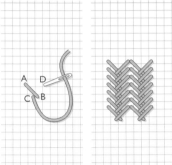

FISHBONE *stitch*

This stitch covers an area with a pattern of asymmetrical, vertical bands. Double-mesh canvas will give the best results. Use a tapestry needle and start at the top left of the area.

1. Bring the needle to the front of the canvas at A and insert it at B. Bring the needle out at C one hole below B and take it up over the intersection to D (see left part of diagram).

2. Now bring the needle out at E and continue to the bottom of the area.

3. To work the return row, bring the needle out at F and insert it at G. Bring it out at H and insert it at I to make the tie (see right part of diagram).

4. Bring the needle out in the hole above F and continue to the top.

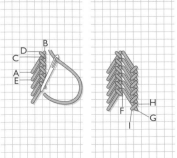

loop stitches

Loop stitches are those in which the thread forms loops above the canvas to give a raised texture to the work. The loops form a raised pile that can sometimes be cut and trimmed to create a velvetlike or carpetlike effect. These stitches can be used for making handmade rugs.
Loop stitches are best worked in wool or heavy, nonstranded cottons. For even results, work over a small rod to make sure that all loops are the same size and use a tapestry needle.

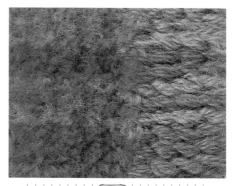

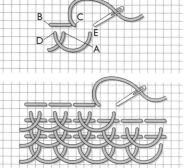

SINGLE KNOTTED *stitch*

1. Begin at the bottom left of the area with the thread on top of the canvas. Insert a tapestry needle at A and leave the tail on top.

2. Bring the needle out at B and insert it at C. Bring it out at D and form a loop by holding the thread with your finger or taking it around a rod. Insert the needle at E (see upper diagram).

3. Bring the needle out at C and continue to the end of the row. Leave a tail of thread on top if you intend to cut the loops later. Begin the second row at the left again (see lower diagram).

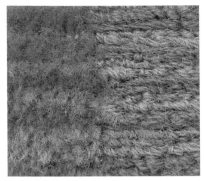

GHIORDES KNOT

(Rya stitch)

This stitch produces raised loops held in place by back stitches (see p. 175). It can be used for making rugs, and the loops can be cut, if desired. On double-mesh canvas, work over each thread separately to produce a denser, stronger version of the stitch. Start at the bottom left of the area.

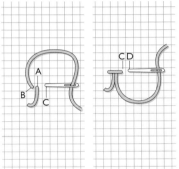

1. Begin with the thread on top of the canvas. Insert a tapestry needle at A and leave a tail on the top (see left part of diagram).

2. Bring the needle out at B. Loop the thread upward, Insert the needle at C and bring it out at A, pulling it through completely to make a back stitch.

3. Loop the thread around downward and hold it with your finger or take it around a rod. Insert the needle at D and bring it out at C. Loop the thread upward, insert the needle into the hole to the right of D and bring it out at C. Pull it through to make a back stitch (see right part of diagram).

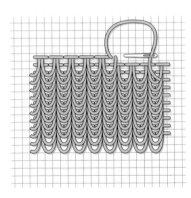

4. Repeat step 3 to the end of the row. Leave a tail of thread on top if you intend to cut the loops later.

5. To work the second row, bring the needle out at the left end, one hole above A, and work as for the first row.

HELPFUL HINT

If you want to cut the loops to create an open pile, wait until the entire area has been stitched. Then cut each loop in the center with a pair of sharp embroidery scissors. Fluff it up and then shear across to even up the pile.

SURREY *stitch*

This stitch produces raised loops held in place with diagonal stitches. It can be used for making rugs and the loops can be cut if desired. On double-mesh canvas, work over each thread separately to produce a denser, stronger version of the stitch. Use a tapestry needle and start at the bottom left of the area.

1. Begin with the thread on top of the canvas. Insert the needle in at A and leave a tail on the top (see top-left diagram).

2. Bring the needle out at B, keeping the tail to the right.

3. Take the thread to the left, looping it around upward. Working within the loop, insert the needle at C and bring it out at A, with the thread still to the left. Pull the thread firmly.

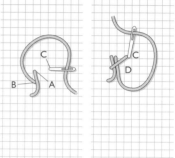

4. Loop the thread downward and to the right and hold it in place with your finger or take it around a rod. Insert the needle at C and bring it out two holes below at D, keeping the thread below the needle (see top-right diagram).

5. Repeat steps 3 and 4 to the end of the row. Leave a tail of thread on top if you intend to cut the loops later.

6. To begin the second row, put the needle in at the left end, two holes above A, and leave a tail, as shown.

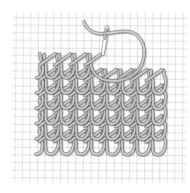

VELVET *stitch*

This stitch produces raised loops held in place with cross-stitches. It can be used for making rugs and the loops can be cut if desired. On double-mesh canvas, work over each thread separately to produce a denser, stronger version of the stitch. Start at the bottom left of the area.

1. Bring a tapestry needle to the front of the canvas at A and insert it at B (see top-left diagram).

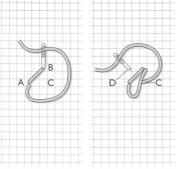

2. Again, bring the needle out at A and loop the thread down and around. Hold it in place with your finger or take it around a rod, and again insert the needle at B.

3. Still retaining the loop, bring the needle out at C, so that the needle is below the thread (see top-right diagram).

4. Continue holding the loop and take the needle across the thread. Insert it at D and bring it out at C, to the right of the thread. Pull the thread firmly to complete the cross-stitch.

5. Continue to the end of the row. Leave a tail of thread on top if you intend to cut the loops later, as shown.

6. To begin the second row, bring the needle out at the left end, at D, and stitch as before.

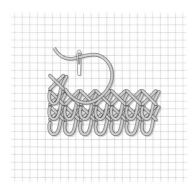

finished
EMBROIDERY

This chapter describes the best methods for displaying, cleaning, and storing your completed embroidery. Following these instructions will help prolong the life of your embroidered piece for as long as possible.

CARING FOR YOUR EMBROIDERY

Cleaning embroidery

Embroidered pieces should not be dry cleaned, as the chemicals used can react with the dyes in the threads. If dry cleaning is essential, always explain this problem to the dry cleaner when submitting the item. If an embroidery piece cannot be washed, marks can sometimes be removed using stain remover, but be sure to test the remover on a scrap of the fabric first.

Canvas work can be cleaned by vacuuming, using an upholstery nozzle and low suction. Pieces that are fragile should be protected by holding a piece of soft netting between the embroidery and the vacuum nozzle. Bind the edges of the netting with tape or fix it to a wooden frame before vacuuming through it.

Washing embroidery

Although washing embroidery can damage it, some pieces will need to be washed occasionally and others, such as clothing and linens, on a regular basis. Following a few guidelines will allow you to keep them in good condition for as long as possible.
- Always wash embroidered pieces by hand, and wash each piece separately.
- Test to ensure the threads are colorfast. Dab a damp cotton ball on the back of the piece, testing each thread color separately. If

any are not colorfast, try not to wash them.
- Use lukewarm water and mild soap. (Avoid harsh detergents.) Do not rub or twist the item.
- Rinse the piece in clear water. If a dye does run, keep rinsing until the water is clear.
- To dry the piece, roll it between two towels and press out the moisture. Then leave it on a towel to dry flat in the shade.

HELPFUL HINT

Embroidery containing true metallic threads should never be washed or dry cleaned. The metallic threads can be cleaned with a soft brush.

Ironing embroidery

Most embroidered pieces will need to be ironed after they are finished to remove creases in the fabric, and certainly after they have been washed. Steam is especially useful for silk threads, as it increases the sheen.
- To iron embroidery, place it facedown on a clean towel and cover it with a clean, damp, colorfast cloth. Use a warm steam iron to press lightly, lifting the iron up and down. The iron should not be dragged across the fabric.
- Ironing preparations and protectors such as spray starch or spray sizing should not be used, as they may cause a chemical reaction with the thread dyes.

Storing embroidery

Fabrics and threads will inevitably deteriorate over time, but there are some simple guidelines for storing your embroidery that will allow you to preserve it in good condition for as long as possible.

● Never fold the item, as the threads at the crease will be weakened. Store it flat or roll it, right side out in clean fabric, such as muslin (cheesecloth) or acid-free tissue paper. Cloth bags are ideal for many items. Natural fibers may sweat, so plastic bags and containers, which trap moisture, should not be used to store embroidered pieces. If an item is too large to be stored without being folded, use tissue paper in the folds and shake it out and refold it every three months.

● Store embroidery in a dry, dark place such as a drawer, cupboard, or acid-free cardboard box. Protect pieces with wool threads by including a natural insect repellent, such as lavender, cedar chips, or camphor, but keep the repellent out of direct contact with the embroidered piece.

DISPLAYING EMBROIDERY

Embroidery that will be displayed as wall hangings, pictures, pillows, or other upholstery should be mounted or hung correctly to prevent distortion and damage.

Mounting embroidery

After pressing and blocking (see p. 14), embroidered pieces can be mounted on a stretcher frame or over board for display or before being framed. When mounting embroidery, never use glue or tape, as they may react with the fabric and mark it or cause deterioration of the fibers.

Using board

A piece of board or strong, acid-free card-board can be used for mounting embroidery. If desired, a piece of batting can be stapled to the board to provide extra protection for the embroidery. The batting should continue around to the backside of the board.

Lay the embroidery facedown on a table and center the board (batting side down) on top of it. Fold opposite sides of the embroidered piece over the board and secure them with pins. Lace the two sides together using a needle and strong thread as shown in the top-right diagram. Start and end with a single back stitch. Fold over the other two sides and repeat.

Turn the board over and check to be sure that the embroidery is centered. Adjust the lacing if necessary, and then finish off the lacing threads with several back stitches.

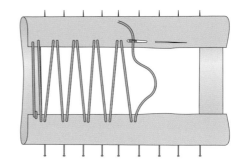

Lace the sides together with strong thread.

Using a stretcher frame

Canvas work is often mounted on a stretcher frame. Choose a frame that is slightly smaller than the embroidered area. Lay the work facedown and place the frame on top of it.

Staple the edges to the frame.

Before finally framing a piece of embroidery, try displaying it in several frames to be certain you are happy with the results.

Bring the canvas edges around the frame and fasten them in the center of each side with one staple. Then begin at the center of each side and work out toward the corners. Make sure that the work is pulled firmly around the frame, but do not distort it.

Framing embroidery

Follow these guidelines for framing embroidery effectively.

● Select a frame to fit the mounted embroidery: The window should be a little smaller than the stretcher or board, so that the edges do not show.

● If glass is to be used, the frame should have a stepped rebate, so that the glass does not rest directly on the embroidery, or it should be large enough so that an acid-free cardboard mount can be included.

● Be sure to use glass that is nonreflective. Conservation glass screens out ultraviolet light that can damage the fabric. Seal the back to prevent condensation.

The texture of the work will be better displayed if glass is not used, but in that case, the work will eventually require cleaning.

Lining embroidery

Unframed hangings and items such as rugs or covers should be lined to prevent threads from catching and unraveling and to help prevent distortion during use.

Press and block the item as usual. Trim unworked canvas or extra fabric to about 1¼ in. (3 cm) deep all around and fold it to the wrong side to make a hem. Slip stitch the hem in place. If the piece was worked on canvas, threads will be visible at the edge. You should overstitch them with thread to match the embroidery.

Cut lining fabric to fit 2 in. (5 cm) larger all around than the embroidery and place it on the embroidery with wrong sides together. Slip stitch around the edges to join the pieces. If desired, a layer of interlining or thin

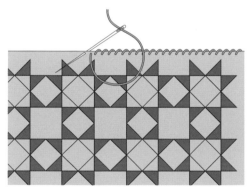

Overstitch the edges of canvas to match the embroidery.

batting may be stitched to the back of the lining before it is added. Leave the bottom edge of a hanging open and hang it for a few days before completing the stitching.

HELPFUL HINT

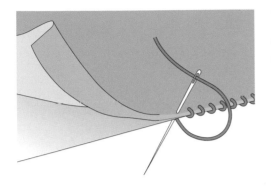

Stitch the lining to the back of the embroidery.

If you are having your embroidery framed professionally, look for a framer who is experienced with embroidery. Many picture framers are not accustomed to blocking and otherwise preparing hand-stitched fabric.

Hanging embroidery

Embroidery may be hung without being framed. First press, block, and line the piece.

Sleeve method

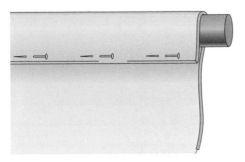

Make a sleeve to fit the pole.

To hang an embroidered piece from a rod, stitch a strong piece of cotton fabric to the top of the embroidery, and make a sleeve to fit the rod.

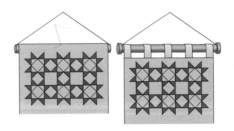

Use a continuous sleeve or a series of tabs to hang the embroidery.

Cut a groove around each end of the rod, or drill a hole through each end, and attach cord. If preferred, a number of fabric tabs can be used instead of a continuous sleeve, as shown.

Large items

Larger, heavier pieces are best hung from a timber batten attached to the wall. Cut a piece of Velcro strip to the same length as the width of the embroidery. Cut a strip of sturdy cotton fabric to the same length and stitch the fuzzy side of the Velcro to the cotton strip. Then stitch the cotton along the top of the back of the embroidery. Tack or staple the other side of the Velcro to the timber batten.

GLOSSARY

Aida cloth evenly woven fabric with threads in squares; used for counted-thread embroidery, especially cross-stitch.

Assisi work counted-thread embroidery technique in which the motif is left unstitched and the background covered with cross-stitch.

bargello work technique in which different shades of thread and long stitches are used to create flamelike or zigzag patterns; also known as Florentine stitch.

batiste fine, plainweave cotton fabric.

batting soft padding made from natural or synthetic fibers; used in quilting and for mounting embroidery.

blackwork counted-thread embroidery technique that uses small, straight stitches; usually worked with black thread on white fabric.

blocking stretching distorted fabric or canvas to return it to its original shape.

broderie anglaise cutwork technique characterized by eyelets and scalloped edges.

bullion metallic thread coiled like a spring, with a hollow center.

candlewick embroidery embroidery technique in which knot stitches are used to outline the design.

canvas woven mesh with the same number of evenly spaced warp and weft threads.

colorfast dye will not run when fabrics and threads are dampened or immersed in water.

couché rentré couching method in which the anchoring stitches are pulled tight, so that the laid thread appears to form stitches.

couching laying a thread on the surface of the fabric and anchoring it by stitching with another thread.

count the number of threads per 1 in. (2.5 cm) in evenweave fabric.

counted-thread embroidery embroidery worked on evenweave fabric by counting the number of threads.

crewel work surface embroidery worked with fine wool threads to form curvilinear plant and animal motifs.

cutwork embroidery technique in which areas of the fabric are cut away after stitching.

damask reversible cotton, silk, linen, or wool fabric with woven patterns.

drawn-thread work counted-thread embroidery technique in which threads are drawn from the fabric, leaving threads in only one direction.

dressmaker's carbon paper waxed carbon paper used for marking patterns and designs; will not smudge like ordinary carbon paper.

evenweave fabric fabric with the same number of evenly spaced warp and weft threads; used for counted-thread embroidery.

eyelet small hole edged with stitches.

fabric material produced by weaving together horizontal and vertical threads.

Florentine work canvas-work technique in which different shades of thread and long stitches are used to create flamelike or zigzag patterns; also known as bargello.

freestyle embroidery embroidery worked on plainweave fabric following design lines.

gauge the number of threads (or holes) per 1 in. (2.5 cm) in canvas.

gimp metallic thread formed by wrapping gold or silver leaf around a fiber core; heavier than passing thread.

gingham plainweave cotton fabric, usually checked.

Hardanger embroidery cutwork technique worked on evenweave fabric and based on kloster blocks.

Hardanger fabric evenweave fabric used for Hardanger embroidery.

insertion work method of joining two pieces of fabric, using decorative stitches to bridge a gap.

interlining nonwoven fabric placed between two pieces of fabric; used to prevent the fabric from losing its shape.

kloster block a square of five satin stitches; used in Hardanger embroidery.

lawn thin cotton or linen fabric.

linen fabric made from flax; used for evenweave and plainweave fabrics.

lurex thread that incorporates fine metallic filaments, so it resembles metallic thread but is softer.

Madeira work cutwork embroidery technique that uses colored threads.

metallic thread thread made from a metal (gold, silver, aluminium, copper) or other material to resemble metal.

monochrome work embroidery worked in a single color or values of one color.

muslin (cheesecloth) a lightweight cotton fabric.

needlepoint term sometimes used for canvas work, especially when worked in tent stitch.

openwork any embroidery in which threads are removed or drawn apart, including drawn-thread work and pulled-fabric work.

opus anglicanum "English work," a term used for the elaborate and intricate embroideries produced in England during the medieval period.

or nué technique of making pictures using gold laid threads, with the colored anchoring stitches spaced to produce shading and perspective views.

organza lightweight fabric made from cotton, silk, or nylon.

padding fabric, felt, cotton, wool, or other material over which stitches are worked.

passing thread fine metallic thread formed by wrapping gold or silver leaf around a fiber core.

Penelope canvas double-mesh canvas with interlocked threads.

picot ornamental loop or knot on the edge of a line of embroidery.

plainweave fabric fabric in which the weave is not regular or obvious.

plate flat, metallic strip.

plunging technique of taking the ends of couched threads to the back of the work.

ply threads twisted together to make thicker, stronger yarn (e.g., 2-ply yarn consists of two threads).

pulled work counted-thread embroidery technique in which the stitches are pulled tightly to form small holes.

purl metallic thread similar to, but finer than, bullion.

raised work embroidery technique in which stitches sit on top of the fabric and are worked over padding to create a three-dimensional effect.

rayon synthetic fabric or thread made from cellulose.

Renaissance work cutwork technique in which the background areas are cut away.

Richelieu work cutwork embroidery technique characterized by picots and buttonhole bars.

rya pile longer than 1 in. (2.5 cm).

sampler piece of embroidery showing different stitches and embroidery techniques; traditionally produced as a learning exercise or to demonstrate skill.

satin fabric with smooth, glossy surface.

scalloped edged with semicircular curves.

shadow work embroidery technique in which stitches are worked on the wrong side of very lightweight fabric, so that the color shows through.

skein thread or yarn that is not on a spool; sometimes wound so that one end can be pulled out from the encircling paper for use.

slip small piece of fabric added to the main fabric in raised work.

smocking ornamental stitching used to gather fabric.

stabilizer fabric fabric, usually nonwoven, applied to the back of the embroidery fabric to prevent it from losing its shape.

stitch particular method of applying thread to a fabric.

strand one filament or thread of a number forming stranded thread.

stranded thread thread with six strands; can be divided and one or more threads used at a time; also known as embroidery floss.

stump work raised embroidery technique in which stitches are worked over padding, wires or wooden "stumps."

surface embroidery embroidery worked on plainweave fabric (as opposed to counted-thread embroidery.

basting temporary joining of two pieces of fabric with long, loose stitches that are removed after the main stitching.

tapestry name sometimes applied to canvas work; more properly, fabric with a woven pictorial design.

thimble rigid cap placed over a finger to protect it from being pricked by the needle during sewing.

thread fine, cordlike material made by twisting together two or more filaments of plant or animal material.

tramming technique of stitching over a thread laid along the canvas .

voile semitransparent, openweave fabric made from cotton, silk, rayon, or wool.

warp threads threads placed lengthwise, usually vertically, on the loom and held under tension; the weft threads are woven in to make fabric.

waste canvas canvas that can be pulled apart when wet; used for working counted-thread designs on plainweave fabric.

weft threads threads woven into the warp threads to make fabric.

whitework any embroidery worked with white thread on white fabric.

INDEX

A READER'S DIGEST BOOK

First published by Marabout, an imprint of Hachette Livre
Copyright © 2004 Marabout (Hachette Livre)

This edition published by The Reader's Digest Association, Inc.,
by arrangement with Marabout (Hachette Livre)

Copyright © 2006

FOR HACHETTE LIVRE
Publisher: Catie Ziller
Editor: Christine Eslick
Additional Editorial Work: JMS Books LLP
Designer: Michelle Cutler
Embroidery: Jennifer Campbell (surface embroidery and smocking),
Ann-Marie Bakewell (canvas work), Michelle Cutler (front cover, p. 234),
Christine Eslick (p. 37), Marjorie Eslick (pp. 237, 242)
Photography: Ian Hofstetter
Illustrations: Stephen Pollitt

FOR READER'S DIGEST
U.S. Project Editor: Marilyn J. Knowlton
Copy Editor: Mary T. Connell
Canadian Project Editor: Pamela Johnson
Project Designer: George McKeon
Executive Editor, Trade Publishing: Dolores York
President & Publisher, Books & Music: Harold Clarke

Library of Congress Cataloging-in-Publication Data

Campbell, Jennifer, 1950-

    The complete guide to embroidery stitches : photographs, diagrams, and instructions for
over 260 illustrated stitches / embroidery by Jennifer Campbell and Ann-Marie Bakewell.
    p. cm.
Includes index.
ISBN 0-7621-0658-1
1. Embroidery I. Title: Embroidery stitches. II. Bakewell, Ann-Marie. III Title.

TT770.C33 2006
746.44'042--dc22

                                                            2005050773

Address any comments about *Complete Guide to Embroidery Stitches* to:
        The Reader's Digest Association, Inc.
        Adult Trade Publishing
        Reader's Digest Road
        Pleasantville, NY 10570-7000

For more Reader's Digest products and information, visit our websites:
        www.rd.com (in the United States)
        www.readersdigest.ca (in Canada)
        www.readersdigest.com.au (in Australia)
        www.rdasia.com

Printed in Singapore

1 3 5 7 9 10 8 6 4 2